How to Start a Tax Preparation Business

Introduction: How to Start a Juice Business

Welcome to the exciting journey of starting your own juice business! In today's health-conscious world, the demand for fresh, nutritious beverages continues to grow, presenting a lucrative opportunity for aspiring entrepreneurs. Whether you're passionate about promoting wellness through delicious blends of fruits and vegetables or you see a gap in your local market for quality juice products, this book is your comprehensive guide to navigating the nuances of launching and running a successful juice business.

Exploring Every Aspect:

This book covers everything you need to know, from initial planning and market research to sourcing ingredients, creating a compelling menu, setting up operations, and marketing your juices effectively. Each chapter is designed to provide practical insights, expert tips, and actionable steps to help you build a thriving juice business that not only meets but exceeds customer expectations.

What to Expect:

Throughout the chapters, we'll delve into crucial topics such as developing unique recipes, ensuring product quality and safety, managing finances, establishing a strong brand presence, and expanding your business sustainably. Whether you're starting small with a juice bar or dreaming of scaling up to distribute your products regionally, this book will equip you with the knowledge and strategies to navigate every stage of your entrepreneurial journey.

Embrace the Journey:

Starting a juice business is more than just selling beverages—it's about passion, innovation, and making a positive impact on the health and well-being of your customers. By embracing creativity, staying informed about industry trends, and fostering a strong connection with your community, you'll not only build a successful business but also contribute to a healthier, happier world one refreshing sip at a time.

Copyright © 2024

All rights reserved. No part of this book may be reproduced in any form or by any electronic or mechanical means, including information storage and retrieval systems, without permission in writing from the publisher, except by a reviewer, who may quote brief passages in a review.

The information contained in this book is for general information purposes only. The information is provided by naciro and while we endeavor to keep the information up to date and correct, we make no representations or warranties of any kind, express or implied, about the completeness, accuracy, reliability, suitability or availability with respect to the book or the information, products, services, or related graphics contained in the book for any purpose. Any reliance you place on such information is therefore strictly at your own risk.

All trademarks and registered trademarks are the property of their respective owners and are used in this book only for identification and explanation.

Permission to use copyrighted material in this book should be obtained from the copyright owner or the publisher.

This book is not intended to provide medical, legal, or financial advice, and the author and publisher specifically disclaim any liability for any loss or damage caused or alleged to be caused directly or indirectly by the information in this book.

Naciro and the publisher of this book do not endorse or recommend any commercial products, processes, or services. The views and opinions of authors expressed in this book do not necessarily state or reflect those of the publisher of this book.

In today's complex financial landscape, starting a tax preparation business can be a lucrative venture for those with a knack for numbers and a passion for helping others navigate the intricacies of taxation. As governments continually revise tax laws and regulations, individuals and businesses alike seek knowledgeable professionals to ensure compliance and maximize their financial returns. This book, "How to Start a Tax Preparation Business," serves as your comprehensive guide to launching and growing a successful tax service enterprise.

Chapter 2: Developing Your Tax Expertise

Welcome to the exciting journey of becoming a proficient tax preparer! Whether you're starting fresh or looking to refine your skills, this chapter will guide you through the essential steps to develop the expertise necessary to excel in the tax preparation industry.

Assessing Your Skills and Knowledge

Before diving into the technical aspects of tax preparation, take some time for self-assessment. Evaluate your existing skills in mathematics, attention to detail, and analytical thinking. These foundational skills form the bedrock of a successful tax preparer. If you find areas where you can improve, consider taking relevant courses or workshops to strengthen these skills.

Education and Certification Requirements

While not always mandatory, formal education and certifications can significantly enhance your credibility and marketability as a tax preparer. Many successful tax professionals hold degrees in accounting, finance, or related fields. Additionally, obtaining certifications such as Enrolled Agent (EA), Certified Public Accountant (CPA), or Accredited Tax Preparer (ATP) can open doors to higher-paying opportunities and broader client trust.

Choosing the Right Training Program

Investing in quality training is crucial for staying updated with tax laws and regulations. Look for reputable tax preparation courses or programs offered by professional organizations, community colleges, or online platforms. These programs typically cover tax theory, practical application, and preparation for certification exams.

Gaining Practical Experience

Theory is invaluable, but practical experience is where you truly hone your skills. Consider internships or entry-level positions at tax preparation firms to gain hands-on experience. This exposure not only familiarizes you with different tax scenarios but also allows you to observe seasoned professionals in action and learn best practices.

Specializing in Niche Markets

As you gain experience, consider specializing in specific niche markets. Whether it's small businesses, expatriates, freelancers, or retirees, niche specialization can set you apart from generalist tax preparers. Specialization allows you to deepen your expertise in specific tax issues relevant to your chosen market, making you a sought-after expert in your field.

Continuous Learning and Professional Development

The tax landscape is constantly evolving, with new laws, regulations, and technologies shaping the industry. Commit to lifelong learning by staying updated with industry trends, attending seminars, and participating in professional development programs. This proactive approach not only enhances your knowledge but also demonstrates your commitment to providing top-notch service to your clients.

Networking and Mentorship

Networking within the tax preparation community can provide invaluable support and insights. Join professional associations, attend industry conferences, and connect with fellow tax professionals. Seeking mentorship from experienced practitioners can also accelerate your learning curve and provide guidance on navigating challenges unique to the tax preparation industry.

Developing Soft Skills

Beyond technical expertise, developing strong interpersonal skills is crucial in tax preparation. Effective communication, empathy, and the ability to simplify complex tax concepts for clients are key attributes of successful tax preparers. Practice active listening and cultivate a client-centric approach to build trust and loyalty with your clientele.

Embracing Technology

Technology is revolutionizing tax preparation, from cloud-based software to automated data entry tools. Embrace these advancements to streamline your workflow, improve accuracy, and enhance client satisfaction. Familiarize yourself with popular tax preparation software and explore how integrating technology can optimize your business operations.

Ethical Standards and Professional Conduct

Maintaining high ethical standards is non-negotiable in the tax preparation profession. Uphold client confidentiality, avoid conflicts of interest, and adhere to professional codes of conduct. Your reputation for integrity and trustworthiness is paramount in building long-lasting client relationships and sustaining a successful tax preparation business.

Conclusion

Developing your tax expertise is a continuous journey that requires dedication, ongoing learning, and a passion for helping others navigate the complexities of taxation. By investing in your skills, staying updated with industry trends, and fostering strong client relationships, you're laying a solid foundation for a rewarding career as a proficient tax preparer. Embrace the challenges and opportunities that come with mastering tax preparation, and you'll be well on your way to achieving professional success in this dynamic field.

Chapter 3: Business Planning Essentials

Welcome to the crucial phase of laying the groundwork for your tax preparation business! This chapter dives into the essentials of business planning, helping you build a solid foundation for your entrepreneurial journey.

Understanding Your Market

Begin by researching your target market. Identify the demographic profiles of potential clients, understand their needs, and assess the demand for tax preparation services in your area. This knowledge will guide your business strategy and marketing efforts.

Defining Your Services

Clearly define the services you'll offer. Will you focus on individual tax returns, small businesses, or both? Consider additional services like tax planning, audit assistance, or financial consulting to diversify your offerings and attract a broader client base.

Crafting a Business Plan

A well-crafted business plan serves as your roadmap to success. Outline your business goals, target market, competitive analysis, marketing strategies, financial projections, and operational plan. A comprehensive business plan not only clarifies your vision but also helps secure funding if needed.

Setting SMART Goals

Set specific, measurable, achievable, relevant, and time-bound (SMART) goals for your tax preparation business. Whether it's acquiring a certain number of clients within the first year or achieving a revenue milestone, SMART goals provide clarity and motivation to track your progress.

Budgeting and Financial Planning

Develop a realistic budget and financial plan for your business. Consider startup costs, ongoing expenses (rent, utilities, software), employee salaries (if applicable), and potential revenue streams. Monitoring your finances closely ensures financial stability and informs strategic decisions.

Choosing a Business Structure

Select a business structure that suits your needs and offers legal and tax benefits. Options include sole proprietorship, partnership, LLC, or S corporation. Consult with a legal or financial advisor to understand the implications of each structure and choose the best fit for your tax preparation business.

Securing Licenses and Permits

Ensure compliance with regulatory requirements by obtaining necessary licenses and permits. Depending on your location, this may include a business license, tax preparer registration, or state-specific permits. Research local regulations to avoid legal issues and operate your business smoothly.

Building Your Brand

Your brand is more than just a logo; it represents your business's identity and values. Develop a compelling brand message that resonates with your target audience. Create a professional website, establish a presence on social media platforms, and invest in marketing strategies to build brand awareness and attract clients.

Creating a Marketing Strategy

Craft a marketing strategy to reach and engage potential clients effectively. Utilize a mix of online and offline tactics such as social media marketing, content creation (blogs, articles), networking events, and referrals. Consistent marketing efforts will help you establish credibility and grow your client base over time.

Evaluating Risk and Mitigation Strategies

Identify potential risks to your business, such as economic downturns, cybersecurity threats, or legal challenges. Develop mitigation strategies to minimize these risks, such as insurance coverage, data security protocols, and contingency plans. Being prepared ensures resilience in the face of challenges.

Conclusion

Business planning is a foundational step in launching and growing your tax preparation business. By conducting thorough market research, defining your services, crafting a robust business plan, and implementing effective marketing strategies, you're setting yourself up for success. Stay adaptable, monitor your progress against goals, and continue refining your strategies to achieve long-term business growth and client satisfaction.

Chapter 4: Legal and Regulatory Requirements

Congratulations on taking the next step in starting your tax preparation business! In this chapter, we'll navigate the maze of legal and regulatory requirements essential for ensuring compliance and laying a solid legal foundation for your venture.

Understanding Legal Structures

One of the first decisions you'll face is choosing a legal structure for your business. The most common options for tax preparation businesses include:

1. Sole Proprietorship: This is the simplest form, where you are the sole owner of the business. You have complete control over operations and receive all profits but also bear full responsibility for debts and liabilities.

2. Partnership: If you're starting the business with others, a partnership allows you to share profits, responsibilities, and liabilities with your partners. It's crucial to have a partnership agreement outlining roles, responsibilities, profit-sharing, and dispute resolution.

3. Limited Liability Company (LLC): An LLC offers limited liability protection to its owners (called members), meaning your personal assets are generally protected from business debts and liabilities. It combines the simplicity of a sole proprietorship with the liability protection of a corporation.

4. Corporation: A corporation is a separate legal entity from its owners (shareholders), providing the highest level of personal liability protection. It involves more complex legal and tax requirements but can offer tax advantages and facilitate raising capital through the sale of shares.

Choosing the right legal structure depends on factors like liability protection, tax implications, operational flexibility, and your long-term business goals. Consult with a legal advisor or accountant to determine the best option for your specific circumstances.

Registering Your Business

Once you've chosen a legal structure, you'll need to register your business with the appropriate government authorities. This typically involves:

1. Business Name Registration: Choose a unique and memorable name for your tax preparation business and register it with your state or local government. Ensure the name is not already in use by another business to avoid legal complications.

2. Employer Identification Number (EIN): Obtain an EIN from the IRS, even if you don't have employees. An EIN is necessary for tax filing, opening a business bank account, and hiring employees in the future.

3. State and Local Licenses: Depending on your location, you may need specific licenses or permits to operate a tax preparation business legally. Research and comply with local regulations regarding business licensing, tax preparer registration, and any industry-specific requirements.

Tax Compliance and Regulations

As a tax preparer, compliance with federal, state, and local tax laws is paramount. Stay informed about tax filing deadlines, reporting requirements, and changes in tax legislation that may impact your clients. Familiarize yourself with:

1. IRS Regulations: Understand IRS rules and guidelines governing tax preparation, including preparer tax identification numbers (PTINs), electronic filing requirements, and taxpayer privacy regulations (e.g., IRS Publication 4557, Safeguarding Taxpayer Data).

2. State Tax Laws: Each state may have its own tax laws and regulations that affect how you prepare and file state income tax returns for your clients. Be aware of state-specific requirements and keep abreast of any updates or changes.

3. Professional Standards and Ethics: Adhere to professional standards and ethical guidelines set forth by organizations such as the IRS, National Association of Tax Professionals (NATP), and American Institute of CPAs (AICPA). Maintain confidentiality, avoid conflicts of interest, and uphold the integrity of the tax preparation process.

Insurance Coverage

Protect your business from potential risks with adequate insurance coverage. Consider:

1. Professional Liability Insurance: Also known as errors and omissions (E&O) insurance, this coverage protects you from claims of negligence or mistakes in your tax preparation services.

2. General Liability Insurance: This insurance provides coverage for third-party claims of bodily injury, property damage, or personal injury arising from your business operations.

3. Cyber Liability Insurance: Safeguard against data breaches and cyberattacks that could compromise sensitive client information. Cyber liability insurance covers costs associated with data recovery, legal fees, and notification expenses.

Consult with an insurance agent specializing in small businesses to assess your insurance needs and customize a policy that provides comprehensive coverage for your tax preparation business.

Client Contracts and Engagement Letters

Establish clear expectations and protect your interests with written client contracts or engagement letters. These documents outline the scope of services, fees, responsibilities, and terms of engagement between you and your clients. A well-drafted contract helps prevent misunderstandings, defines boundaries, and provides recourse in case of disputes.

Record Keeping and Documentation

Maintain accurate records of all financial transactions, client interactions, and tax filings. Proper record keeping not only facilitates compliance with tax laws and regulations but also supports business planning, financial analysis, and decision-making. Use reliable accounting software to track income, expenses, invoices, and receipts efficiently.

Conclusion

Navigating the legal and regulatory landscape may seem daunting, but with thorough preparation and attention to detail, you can establish a strong legal foundation for your tax preparation business. By choosing the right legal structure, registering your business, ensuring tax compliance, obtaining necessary licenses and insurance, and implementing robust record-keeping practices, you're setting the stage for long-term success and compliance in the dynamic field of tax preparation. Stay informed about regulatory updates, seek professional advice when needed, and prioritize ethical practices to build trust and credibility with your clients and stakeholders.

Chapter 5: Choosing Your Business Structure

Welcome to the critical decision-making process of choosing the right business structure for your tax preparation business! This chapter will guide you through the options available and help you select the structure that aligns with your goals, preferences, and operational needs.

Importance of Choosing the Right Business Structure

Selecting the appropriate business structure is more than just a legal formality; it profoundly impacts your business operations, taxes, liability, and ability to raise capital. Each structure offers unique advantages and considerations, so it's essential to weigh your options carefully before making a decision.

Common Business Structures for Tax Preparation Businesses

Let's explore the most common business structures and their key characteristics:

1. Sole Proprietorship:

Overview: A sole proprietorship is the simplest and most common structure for small businesses. As the sole owner, you have complete control over the business and its operations.

Advantages:

- Easy and inexpensive to set up.
- Full control over decision-making.
- Simplified tax filing (profits and losses reported on your personal tax return).

Considerations:

- Unlimited personal liability for business debts and obligations.
- Limited ability to raise capital compared to other structures.
- Potential challenges in attracting clients who prefer working with more established entities.

2. Partnership:

Overview: A partnership involves two or more individuals sharing ownership and responsibility for the business. Partners contribute capital, share profits and losses, and jointly manage operations.

Advantages:

- Shared decision-making and workload.
- Access to additional capital and resources through pooled finances.
- Flexible profit-sharing arrangements based on partnership agreement.

Considerations:

- Shared liability among partners for business debts and obligations.
- Potential for disagreements and conflicts over decision-making.
- Each partner's actions can impact the business and affect others' liabilities.

3. Limited Liability Company (LLC):

Overview: An LLC combines the pass-through taxation of a partnership or sole proprietorship with the limited liability protection of a corporation. LLCs are increasingly popular among small businesses due to their flexibility and protection.

Advantages:

- Limited liability protection for owners' personal assets.
- Flexible management structure (can be managed by members or appoint managers).
- Pass-through taxation (profits and losses reported on owners' personal tax returns).

Considerations:

- More complex and costly to establish compared to sole proprietorships or partnerships.
- State-specific regulations and annual reporting requirements.
- Potential for self-employment taxes on income distributions.

4. Corporation:

Overview: A corporation is a separate legal entity from its owners (shareholders), offering the highest level of personal liability protection.

Advantages:

- Limited liability protection shields personal assets from business debts and liabilities.
- Ability to raise capital by selling shares of stock.
- Potential tax advantages, including deductions for employee benefits.

Considerations:

- More complex to form and maintain (requires articles of incorporation, bylaws, shareholder meetings).
- Double taxation: Corporate profits are taxed at the corporate level, and dividends are taxed when distributed to shareholders.
- Strict regulatory requirements and compliance obligations.

Factors to Consider When Choosing a Business Structure

When deciding on a business structure for your tax preparation business, consider the following factors:

1. Liability Protection: Evaluate your exposure to business risks and the level of personal asset protection you need. LLCs and corporations offer limited liability, shielding personal assets from business debts and lawsuits.

2. Tax Implications: Assess the tax advantages and requirements associated with each structure. Consult with a tax advisor to understand how each structure impacts your tax obligations, deductions, and potential for self-employment taxes.

3. Operational Flexibility: Consider how each structure aligns with your business goals and operational needs. Sole proprietorships and partnerships offer simplicity and flexibility in management, while LLCs and corporations provide more formal structures for growth and scalability.

4. Long-Term Goals: Reflect on your long-term business goals, such as growth, succession planning, and attracting investors. Your chosen structure should support these objectives and accommodate future changes in ownership or business direction.

Steps to Establish Your Chosen Business Structure

Once you've chosen a business structure that meets your needs, follow these steps to establish your tax preparation business:

1. Name Registration: Choose a unique and memorable name for your business and ensure it complies with state regulations. Register your business name with the appropriate state or local authorities.

2. Registration and Licenses: Obtain any necessary licenses, permits, or registrations required for operating a tax preparation business in your locality. This may include tax preparer registration, business licenses, and permits for handling sensitive client information.

3. IRS Requirements: Obtain an Employer Identification Number (EIN) from the IRS, even if you don't have employees. An EIN is necessary for tax filing, opening a business bank account, and hiring employees in the future.

4. Drafting Legal Documents: Depending on your chosen structure, prepare legal documents such as articles of incorporation (for corporations), partnership agreements (for partnerships), or operating agreements (for LLCs). These documents outline ownership rights, management structure, profit-sharing arrangements, and operational guidelines.

5. Tax and Accounting Systems: Set up accounting systems and procedures to track income, expenses, and tax obligations. Consider investing in accounting software that integrates with tax preparation tools to streamline financial management and reporting.

Conclusion

Choosing the right business structure is a pivotal decision that sets the framework for your tax preparation business's legal, financial, and operational success. By carefully evaluating your options, considering factors such as liability protection, tax implications, operational flexibility, and long-term goals, you can make an informed choice that supports your entrepreneurial journey. Seek professional advice from legal and tax advisors to navigate complexities and ensure compliance with regulatory requirements. With a solid business structure in place, you're well-positioned to pursue growth opportunities, attract clients, and achieve your business objectives in the dynamic field of tax preparation.

Chapter 6: Setting Up Your Office

Welcome to the chapter dedicated to setting up your office for your tax preparation business! Creating a functional and inviting workspace is crucial for efficiency, professionalism, and client satisfaction. Whether you're starting from scratch or refining your existing setup, this chapter will guide you through the essentials of designing a productive office environment.

Designing Your Workspace

Your office environment plays a significant role in your productivity and client perception. Consider the following aspects when designing your workspace:

1. Location: Choose a location that is convenient for your clients and aligns with your budget. Options may include a home office, leased commercial space, or a shared office arrangement. Ensure accessibility, ample parking, and a professional atmosphere that instills confidence in your clients.

2. Layout: Optimize your office layout for efficiency and workflow. Designate separate areas for client consultations, workspace for tax preparation, and storage of documents and supplies. Ensure ergonomic furniture and adequate lighting to enhance comfort and productivity.

3. Technology Integration: Invest in essential technology tools for tax preparation, such as computers, printers, scanners, and high-speed internet. Consider cloud-based software solutions for secure document storage, client communication, and collaboration with remote team members or clients.

4. Client Comfort: Create a welcoming environment for client meetings. Provide comfortable seating, refreshments, and a clean, organized workspace that reflects professionalism and attention to detail. Consider privacy measures to protect sensitive client information during consultations.

5. Branding and Décor: Incorporate your branding elements into the office décor, including your logo, color scheme, and marketing materials. A cohesive visual identity reinforces your brand image and creates a memorable experience for clients visiting your office.

Equipping Your Office

Equip your office with essential tools and supplies to support your daily operations:

1. Tax Preparation Software: Choose reputable tax preparation software that meets your business needs and integrates with your accounting systems. Look for features such as electronic filing, data security measures, and compatibility with IRS requirements.

2. Office Supplies: Stock up on basic office supplies, including paper, pens, folders, binders, envelopes, and notepads. Maintain an organized inventory to facilitate efficient document management and client communications.

3. Security Measures: Implement robust security measures to protect client data and confidential information. Install antivirus software, encryption tools for sensitive files, and secure backup systems to prevent data loss or breaches.

4. Communication Tools: Establish effective communication channels with clients, including phone systems, email accounts, and secure messaging platforms. Ensure prompt responsiveness to client inquiries and streamline appointment scheduling and reminders.

5. Compliance Resources: Stay updated with IRS publications, tax forms, and regulatory guidelines relevant to your tax preparation business. Maintain a library of reference materials and resources to support accurate and compliant tax filings for your clients.

Establishing a Digital Presence

In today's digital age, a professional online presence is essential for attracting clients and building credibility. Consider the following steps to establish and enhance your digital footprint:

1. Professional Website: Create a user-friendly website that showcases your services, expertise, client testimonials, and contact information. Optimize your website for search engines (SEO) to increase visibility and attract organic traffic.

2. Social Media Presence: Leverage social media platforms such as LinkedIn, Facebook, and Twitter to engage with potential clients, share industry insights, and promote your services. Maintain an active presence by posting relevant content and participating in professional networks.

3. Online Reviews and Testimonials: Encourage satisfied clients to leave positive reviews and testimonials on your website, social media profiles, and industry-specific platforms. Positive feedback enhances your reputation and credibility among prospective clients.

4. Digital Marketing Strategies: Implement targeted digital marketing strategies, such as pay-per-click (PPC) advertising, content marketing (blogs, articles), and email campaigns. Monitor campaign performance and adjust strategies to maximize return on investment (ROI) and client acquisition.

Operational Efficiency and Client Service

Focus on operational efficiency and exceptional client service to differentiate your tax preparation business:

1. Streamlined Processes: Develop standardized processes for client intake, data collection, tax preparation, and filing. Use checklist templates and workflow automation tools to minimize errors and ensure consistency in service delivery.

2. Client Relationship Management: Cultivate strong client relationships through proactive communication, personalized service, and responsiveness to client needs. Maintain detailed client records and notes to provide tailored recommendations and anticipate future tax planning opportunities.

3. Professional Development: Commit to continuous learning and professional development to stay updated with tax laws, industry trends, and technological advancements. Attend workshops, webinars, and industry conferences to expand your knowledge and enhance your expertise as a tax professional.

Conclusion

Setting up your office is a pivotal step in establishing a successful tax preparation business. By designing a functional workspace, equipping your office with essential tools and technology, establishing a digital presence, and prioritizing operational efficiency and client service, you're laying a solid foundation for growth and client satisfaction. Embrace creativity, attention to detail, and a client-centric approach to create a professional environment that reflects your commitment to excellence in tax preparation. With a well-equipped and inviting office, you're prepared to deliver exceptional service, build lasting client relationships, and achieve your entrepreneurial goals in the dynamic field of tax preparation.

Chapter 7: Marketing Your Tax Preparation Business

Welcome to the exciting world of marketing your tax preparation business! Effective marketing is essential for attracting clients, establishing credibility, and growing your business. This chapter explores key strategies and tactics to promote your services, reach your target audience, and differentiate yourself in the competitive tax preparation industry.

Understanding Your Target Audience

Before diving into marketing tactics, it's crucial to understand your target audience—the individuals or businesses most likely to need your tax preparation services. Consider demographics (age, income, occupation), psychographics (attitudes, values, behaviors), and geographic location to tailor your marketing efforts effectively.

1. Identifying Client Needs: What are the specific tax-related challenges or pain points your target audience faces? Understanding these needs enables you to position your services as solutions that address their concerns and provide value.

2. Competitive Analysis: Research competitors in your local area or niche market. Identify their strengths, weaknesses, pricing strategies, and unique selling propositions (USPs). Differentiate your services by highlighting what sets you apart and appeals to your target audience.

Developing Your Unique Selling Proposition (USP)

A compelling Unique Selling Proposition (USP) defines what makes your tax preparation services unique and why clients should choose you over competitors. Consider the following elements when crafting your USP:

1. Specialized Expertise: Highlight any specialized knowledge or certifications (e.g., CPA, Enrolled Agent) that distinguish you as a trusted tax professional in your niche.

2. Personalized Service: Emphasize your commitment to personalized service, attention to detail, and client-focused approach. Demonstrate how you go above and beyond to meet client expectations and deliver exceptional results.

3. Value Proposition: Clearly communicate the benefits and value clients receive by choosing your services, such as maximizing deductions, minimizing tax liabilities, and ensuring compliance with tax laws.

Building Your Brand Identity

Your brand identity encompasses the visual elements, messaging, and values that define your tax preparation business. Develop a cohesive brand identity to strengthen recognition and establish a memorable presence in the market:

1. Logo and Visual Branding: Create a professional logo and choose a color palette that reflects your brand personality and appeals to your target audience. Consistently use these elements across all marketing materials and platforms.

2. Brand Voice: Define your brand voice—how you communicate with clients and prospects. Whether it's friendly and approachable or authoritative and knowledgeable, maintain a consistent tone that resonates with your audience.

3. Brand Story: Share your journey, values, and passion for helping clients navigate tax complexities. Craft a compelling brand story that connects emotionally with clients and underscores your credibility as a trusted advisor.

Crafting Your Marketing Strategy

A well-rounded marketing strategy combines various tactics to reach and engage your target audience effectively. Consider the following strategies to promote your tax preparation business:

1. Website Optimization: Your website serves as the hub of your online presence. Ensure it is mobile-friendly, easy to navigate, and optimized for search engines (SEO). Include clear calls-to-action (CTAs) prompting visitors to contact you or schedule a consultation.

2. Content Marketing: Create valuable content that educates and informs your audience about tax-related topics, changes in tax laws, money-saving tips, and industry insights. Publish blog posts, articles, infographics, and videos to establish thought leadership and attract organic traffic.

3. Social Media Marketing: Leverage social media platforms (e.g., LinkedIn, Facebook, Twitter) to engage with potential clients, share informative content, and promote your services. Participate in industry groups, answer tax-related questions, and showcase client testimonials to build credibility.

4. Email Marketing: Build an email list of current and prospective clients and send regular newsletters, updates, and personalized offers. Use email marketing automation to nurture leads, encourage repeat business, and stay top-of-mind during tax season and throughout the year.

5. Networking and Referrals: Establish relationships with complementary businesses (e.g., financial advisors, attorneys) and participate in local networking events, chamber of commerce meetings, and industry conferences. Encourage satisfied clients to refer friends, family, and colleagues to your services.

Leveraging Online Reviews and Testimonials

Positive reviews and testimonials from satisfied clients can significantly influence prospective clients' decision to choose your tax preparation services. Encourage clients to leave feedback on your website, social media profiles, and industry-specific review platforms. Respond promptly to reviews, whether positive or negative, to demonstrate your commitment to client satisfaction and continuous improvement.

Monitoring and Measuring Success

Monitor the performance of your marketing efforts using key performance indicators (KPIs) such as website traffic, conversion rates, client acquisition cost, and return on investment (ROI). Analyze data regularly to identify successful strategies, optimize campaigns, and adjust tactics as needed to achieve your marketing goals.

Conclusion

Marketing your tax preparation business is a dynamic and ongoing process that requires strategic planning, creativity, and a client-centric approach. By understanding your target audience, developing a compelling USP, building a strong brand identity, and implementing a diverse marketing strategy, you can effectively promote your services, attract new clients, and foster long-term relationships. Stay adaptable, embrace digital marketing tools and trends, and continuously refine your approach to maximize visibility, credibility, and business growth in the competitive tax preparation industry.

Chapter 8: Client Relationship Management

Welcome to the chapter dedicated to mastering client relationship management (CRM) for your tax preparation business! Building strong relationships with your clients is crucial not only for client satisfaction but also for business growth and sustainability. In this chapter, we'll explore strategies and best practices to enhance client relationships, foster loyalty, and position yourself as a trusted advisor in the field of tax preparation.

The Importance of Client Relationships

Establishing and maintaining positive client relationships is at the heart of every successful tax preparation business. Clients are not just transactions but long-term partners who rely on your expertise and trust you with their financial information. Here's why nurturing client relationships is essential:

1. Trust and Credibility: Clients entrust you with sensitive financial data. Building trust through transparent communication, ethical practices, and consistent service delivery enhances your credibility as a reliable tax professional.

2. Repeat Business and Referrals: Satisfied clients are more likely to return for future tax seasons and refer friends, family, and colleagues to your services. Positive word-of-mouth recommendations can significantly impact your business growth and client acquisition.

3. Client Lifetime Value: Long-term client relationships contribute to your business's stability and profitability. By understanding clients' needs, providing personalized service, and offering value-added solutions, you increase client lifetime value and foster loyalty.

Effective Client Communication

Clear and effective communication forms the foundation of strong client relationships. Adopt these communication strategies to enhance client satisfaction and engagement:

1. Active Listening: Listen attentively to clients' concerns, questions, and financial goals. Demonstrate empathy, ask clarifying questions, and show genuine interest in understanding their unique situations.

2. Transparent and Timely Updates: Keep clients informed about tax law changes, filing deadlines, and updates that may affect their financial planning. Provide proactive communication through newsletters, email updates, or personalized consultations.

3. Accessibility and Responsiveness: Be accessible to clients via multiple communication channels (phone, email, in-person meetings) and respond promptly to inquiries and requests. Prompt responsiveness demonstrates your commitment to client service and builds trust.

4. Educate and Empower: Educate clients about tax planning strategies, deductions, credits, and financial decisions that impact their tax liabilities. Empower clients with knowledge to make informed choices and achieve their financial goals.

Personalized Service and Client Care

Deliver personalized service that exceeds client expectations and reinforces your commitment to their success:

1. Tailored Solutions: Customize your approach based on each client's unique financial situation, goals, and preferences. Offer personalized tax planning advice, optimize deductions, and recommend strategies to minimize tax liabilities.

2. Proactive Tax Planning: Anticipate clients' needs beyond tax season. Offer year-round tax planning services, quarterly reviews, and financial forecasts to help clients make strategic financial decisions and achieve long-term financial stability.

3. Celebrate Milestones: Recognize and celebrate clients' milestones, such as business anniversaries, personal achievements, or financial milestones. Send personalized notes, small tokens of appreciation, or congratulatory messages to strengthen relationships.

4. Client Feedback and Satisfaction: Regularly solicit feedback from clients to gauge satisfaction with your services. Use client surveys, reviews, and testimonials to identify areas for improvement and demonstrate responsiveness to client input.

Leveraging Technology for CRM

Utilize technology tools and platforms to streamline client management and enhance service delivery:

1. CRM Software: Invest in CRM software to manage client relationships, track interactions, and maintain detailed client profiles. CRM systems automate tasks, schedule follow-ups, and centralize client communications for improved efficiency.

2. Secure Client Portals: Implement secure client portals for document sharing, e-signatures, and confidential communication. Ensure compliance with data protection regulations (e.g., GDPR, HIPAA) to safeguard client information and maintain trust.

3. Workflow Automation: Automate repetitive tasks such as appointment scheduling, reminders, and document management. Workflow automation reduces administrative burden, improves accuracy, and allows you to focus on delivering exceptional client service.

Handling Client Challenges and Complaints

Address client challenges and complaints with professionalism and empathy to preserve relationships and uphold your reputation:

1. Active Problem-Solving: Listen actively to client concerns, acknowledge their perspective, and propose solutions to resolve issues promptly. Demonstrate empathy and a commitment to achieving a satisfactory outcome.

2. Transparent Communication: Communicate openly about challenges, delays, or errors. Take ownership of mistakes, apologize sincerely, and outline steps to prevent recurrence. Transparent communication builds trust and reinforces your integrity.

3. Follow-Up and Resolution: Follow up with clients after resolving issues to ensure their satisfaction. Document resolutions, implement corrective actions, and use feedback to enhance service delivery and prevent future issues.

Continuous Improvement and Professional Development

Commit to continuous improvement and ongoing professional development to enhance your skills, knowledge, and client service capabilities:

1. Continuing Education: Stay updated with tax laws, regulations, and industry trends through continuing education courses, seminars, and certifications. Expand your expertise in specialized areas (e.g., estate planning, small business taxes) to better serve diverse client needs.

2. Client-Centric Approach: Embrace a client-centric mindset focused on delivering value, exceeding expectations, and fostering long-term client relationships. Regularly assess client satisfaction, adapt service offerings, and innovate based on client feedback and market trends.

Conclusion

Effective client relationship management is a cornerstone of success in the tax preparation industry. By prioritizing trust, communication, personalized service, and leveraging technology, you can cultivate strong client relationships, enhance client satisfaction, and differentiate your tax preparation business in a competitive market. Invest in client loyalty, embrace feedback as an opportunity for growth, and demonstrate your commitment to delivering exceptional service at every client interaction. With a client-focused approach, you're well-positioned to build a loyal client base, drive business growth, and achieve long-term success as a trusted tax advisor.

Chapter 9: Managing Tax Season Successfully

Welcome to the pivotal chapter on managing tax season successfully for your tax preparation business! Tax season is a busy and crucial time when clients rely on your expertise to navigate complex tax laws and maximize their financial outcomes. This chapter provides practical strategies and tips to streamline operations, enhance client service, and optimize efficiency during the peak tax season.

Preparing for Tax Season

Effective preparation is key to managing tax season smoothly and meeting client expectations. Follow these steps to prepare your tax preparation business for the busy season ahead:

1. **Staffing and Resources:** Evaluate staffing needs based on projected workload and client appointments. Hire seasonal staff, if necessary, or redistribute responsibilities among existing team members to ensure adequate coverage and efficient workflow.

2. **Technology Readiness:** Verify that tax preparation software, hardware, and IT infrastructure are up-to-date and functioning properly. Test software compatibility with IRS updates, secure client portals, and backup systems to prevent disruptions during peak periods.

3. **Client Communication:** Notify clients of upcoming tax deadlines, required documentation, and appointment scheduling options. Use email newsletters, social media updates, and website announcements to inform clients and encourage early preparation.

4. **Workflow Planning:** Develop a detailed workflow plan outlining tasks, deadlines, and responsibilities for each stage of tax preparation (client intake, data collection, review, filing). Establish checkpoints to monitor progress and ensure timely completion of client returns.

Enhancing Client Service During Tax Season

Deliver exceptional client service to build trust, satisfaction, and loyalty during tax season:

1. **Appointment Scheduling:** Implement an online booking system or scheduling software to streamline appointment scheduling and minimize wait times. Offer flexible appointment options, including evenings and weekends, to accommodate clients' schedules.

2. **Client Intake Process:** Standardize the client intake process to collect necessary documentation (W-2s, 1099s, receipts) efficiently. Use secure

document upload portals or digital forms to streamline data collection and minimize errors.

3. Proactive Communication: Keep clients informed about the status of their tax returns, IRS updates, and potential refund timelines. Provide regular updates via email, phone calls, or client portals to demonstrate transparency and alleviate concerns.

4. Education and Guidance: Educate clients about tax law changes, deductions, credits, and strategies to optimize their tax outcomes. Offer personalized advice tailored to each client's financial situation and long-term goals.

Managing Workload and Efficiency

Maximize efficiency and productivity to handle increased workload demands during tax season:

1. Time Management: Prioritize tasks based on deadlines and complexity. Implement time-blocking techniques to allocate dedicated time for client meetings, tax preparation, and review processes. Minimize distractions to maintain focus and productivity.

2. Document Management: Organize client documents systematically using digital filing systems or cloud storage solutions. Label and categorize documents by client name, tax year, and document type for easy retrieval and reference.

3. Quality Assurance: Implement quality control measures, such as peer reviews and accuracy checks, to ensure completeness and accuracy of tax returns. Verify calculations, deductions, and compliance with IRS regulations before finalizing client filings.

4. Client Follow-Up: Schedule post-filing reviews with clients to discuss tax outcomes, address questions, and provide recommendations for future tax planning. Proactively identify opportunities to optimize deductions, minimize tax liabilities, and enhance financial strategies.

Handling Challenges and Client Expectations

Anticipate and address challenges effectively to maintain client satisfaction and uphold service standards:

1. Client Queries and Support: Prepare staff to handle client inquiries, concerns, and support requests promptly and professionally. Provide training on common tax-related issues, FAQs, and IRS procedures to ensure consistent client service delivery.

2. Unexpected Changes: Stay informed about last-minute tax law changes, filing extensions, or IRS updates that may impact client returns. Communicate changes to affected clients promptly and adjust workflows accordingly to accommodate new requirements.

3. Stress Management: Encourage a supportive work environment and promote stress management techniques among team members during peak periods. Foster open communication, celebrate milestones, and recognize team efforts to maintain morale and productivity.

Post-Tax Season Review and Planning

Conduct a thorough review of tax season operations to identify strengths, areas for improvement, and lessons learned:

1. Performance Evaluation: Analyze key performance metrics, such as client satisfaction ratings, turnaround times, and error rates. Compare actual performance against projected goals and benchmarks to assess overall efficiency and effectiveness.

2. Client Feedback: Solicit feedback from clients through surveys, reviews, and post-filing evaluations. Use client insights to identify service enhancements, address concerns, and refine client communication strategies for future tax seasons.

3. Staff Development: Recognize team achievements and provide constructive feedback to support professional growth and development. Offer training opportunities, continuing education courses, and skills enhancement programs to prepare staff for evolving client needs and industry changes.

Conclusion

Successfully managing tax season requires strategic planning, efficient workflows, and a client-focused approach to service delivery. By preparing proactively, enhancing client service, optimizing efficiency, and adapting to challenges, you can navigate the complexities of tax season with confidence and professionalism. Maintain clear communication, prioritize client satisfaction, and leverage technology to streamline operations and deliver exceptional value to clients. With effective preparation and execution, you're well-positioned to achieve operational excellence, foster client loyalty, and sustain long-term success in the competitive tax preparation industry.

Chapter 10: Tax Compliance and Ethics

Welcome to the chapter dedicated to understanding tax compliance and ethics in your tax preparation business! Operating ethically and ensuring compliance with tax laws are fundamental responsibilities for tax professionals. This chapter explores the importance of ethical conduct, regulatory compliance, and best practices to uphold integrity, protect clients' interests, and maintain trust in the tax preparation industry.

Importance of Ethical Conduct

Ethical conduct forms the cornerstone of professional integrity and client trust in the tax preparation profession. By adhering to ethical principles, you demonstrate commitment to fairness, honesty, and accountability in all client interactions. Here's why ethical conduct matters:

1. Client Trust: Clients entrust tax professionals with sensitive financial information. Ethical behavior, such as confidentiality, integrity, and transparency, fosters trust and strengthens client relationships.

2. Industry Reputation: Upholding ethical standards enhances the reputation of your tax preparation business and contributes to a positive perception within the industry. Clients, colleagues, and regulatory bodies recognize ethical practitioners as reliable and trustworthy advisors.

3. Legal Compliance: Compliance with ethical guidelines and regulatory requirements (e.g., IRS Circular 230) is essential to avoid legal repercussions, sanctions, or loss of licensure. Understanding and adhering to ethical standards mitigate risks and protect your business's reputation.

Ethical Principles in Tax Preparation

Adhere to ethical principles that guide professional conduct and decision-making in tax preparation:

1. Integrity: Act with honesty, professionalism, and transparency in all client dealings. Avoid misrepresentation, concealment of information, or conflicts of interest that compromise integrity.

2. Confidentiality: Safeguard client confidentiality by securely storing and handling sensitive financial information. Obtain client consent before disclosing information to third parties, except as required by law.

3. Competence and Due Diligence: Maintain proficiency in tax laws, regulations, and industry standards through ongoing education and professional development. Exercise due diligence in preparing accurate tax returns and providing informed advice to clients.

4. Professionalism: Demonstrate respect, courtesy, and professionalism in interactions with clients, colleagues, and regulatory authorities. Uphold ethical standards in marketing, advertising, and client solicitation practices.

Regulatory Compliance and Responsibilities

Compliance with tax laws and regulatory requirements is essential to protect clients' interests and maintain your professional standing. Understand the following compliance obligations:

1. IRS Regulations: Familiarize yourself with IRS regulations, guidelines, and updates relevant to tax preparation practices. Comply with filing deadlines, reporting requirements, and electronic filing mandates to avoid penalties or audits.

2. State and Local Requirements: Stay informed about state-specific tax laws, licensing requirements, and regulatory frameworks governing tax preparation services. Adhere to local regulations and obtain necessary permits or licenses to operate legally.

3. Anti-Money Laundering (AML) Compliance: Implement anti-money laundering measures to prevent illicit financial activities. Conduct due diligence on clients, identify suspicious transactions, and report suspicious activities to regulatory authorities as required by law.

Best Practices for Ethical Tax Preparation

Implement best practices to uphold ethical standards and promote integrity in your tax preparation business:

1. Client Engagement: Establish clear communication with clients regarding fees, services, and expectations. Provide written engagement letters outlining scope of services, responsibilities, and fee structures to prevent misunderstandings.

2. Document Retention: Maintain accurate and organized records of client information, tax returns, supporting documents, and communications. Adhere to record retention policies to facilitate audits, client inquiries, and compliance reviews.

3. Conflict Resolution: Resolve conflicts of interest or ethical dilemmas promptly and transparently. Disclose potential conflicts to affected parties, seek consensus on resolutions, and document decisions to demonstrate adherence to ethical standards.

4. Continuing Education: Commit to lifelong learning and professional development to stay abreast of evolving tax laws, ethical guidelines, and industry trends. Attend seminars, webinars, and training programs to enhance competence and maintain ethical proficiency.

Ethics in Client Relationships

Navigate ethical considerations in client relationships to protect clients' interests and maintain professional integrity:

1. Informed Consent: Obtain informed consent from clients before initiating tax preparation services or making significant financial decisions on their behalf. Educate clients about potential risks, benefits, and implications of tax strategies.

2. Fee Transparency: Disclose fee structures, billing practices, and payment terms to clients upfront. Avoid hidden fees, excessive charges, or billing practices that may undermine trust or lead to client dissatisfaction.

3. Confidentiality Protocols: Implement robust confidentiality protocols to protect client information from unauthorized access, disclosure, or misuse. Secure electronic communications, encrypt sensitive data, and restrict access to client records.

Upholding Ethical Standards

Promote a culture of ethical conduct and accountability within your tax preparation business:

1. Code of Ethics: Develop and enforce a code of ethics outlining expected standards of conduct, ethical principles, and disciplinary measures for non-compliance. Educate staff on ethical guidelines and encourage adherence to ethical standards in daily operations.

2. Ethical Decision-Making: Foster a collaborative approach to ethical decision-making among staff members. Provide guidance, resources, and ethical frameworks to support informed decision-making and uphold organizational integrity.

3. Compliance Audits: Conduct periodic compliance audits and reviews to assess adherence to ethical standards, regulatory requirements, and internal policies. Identify areas for improvement, implement corrective actions, and monitor ongoing compliance efforts.

Conclusion

Ethical conduct and compliance with tax laws are foundational to the success and credibility of your tax preparation business. By prioritizing integrity, transparency, and professionalism, you strengthen client relationships, mitigate risks, and uphold industry standards. Embrace ethical principles as guiding principles in all aspects of your business operations, from client interactions and regulatory compliance to staff development and organizational culture. With a commitment to ethical excellence, you demonstrate leadership in the tax preparation industry and build a reputation as a trusted advisor clients can rely on for their tax and financial needs.

Chapter 11: Growing Your Tax Preparation Business

Congratulations on reaching the chapter focused on growing your tax preparation business! As you expand your client base, enhance service offerings, and increase revenue, strategic growth becomes essential. This chapter explores proven strategies, actionable insights, and practical steps to scale your tax preparation business effectively and sustainably.

Assessing Your Current Position

Before embarking on growth initiatives, assess your current business position, strengths, and areas for improvement:

1. Client Base Analysis: Review your existing client roster to identify demographics, industries, and referral sources. Analyze client retention rates, satisfaction levels, and profitability to understand your client base's composition and needs.

2. Service Offering Evaluation: Evaluate your current service offerings, pricing structures, and competitive positioning. Identify high-demand services, emerging trends, and opportunities for differentiation in the tax preparation market.

3. Financial Health Check: Conduct a financial analysis to assess revenue streams, profitability margins, and operational costs. Determine key financial metrics (e.g., gross revenue, net profit) to measure business performance and identify areas for financial improvement.

Developing a Growth Strategy

Craft a growth strategy tailored to your business goals, market opportunities, and competitive landscape:

1. Market Research: Conduct market research to identify target markets, industry trends, and competitive benchmarks. Explore opportunities in niche markets (e.g., small businesses, expatriates, high-net-worth individuals) where specialized expertise can add value.

2. Value Proposition Refinement: Refine your unique selling proposition (USP) to differentiate your tax preparation services. Highlight specialized expertise, personalized service, innovative solutions, or industry accolades that resonate with target clients and set you apart from competitors.

3. Client Acquisition Plan: Develop a client acquisition plan outlining lead generation strategies, marketing tactics, and sales channels to attract new clients. Utilize digital marketing (e.g., SEO, social media), networking events, referral programs, and partnerships to expand your client base.

Leveraging Technology and Automation

Invest in technology tools and automation to streamline operations, enhance service delivery, and improve efficiency:

1. Tax Preparation Software: Upgrade to advanced tax preparation software that integrates with client portals, e-signature capabilities, and data analytics. Automate routine tasks (e.g., data entry, document management) to minimize manual errors and accelerate workflow.

2. Client Relationship Management (CRM): Implement a CRM system to manage client interactions, track leads, and nurture relationships throughout the client lifecycle. Utilize CRM data to personalize client communications, identify cross-selling opportunities, and enhance client retention.

3. Cloud Computing: Embrace cloud computing for secure data storage, remote access to client information, and scalability. Leverage cloud-based solutions for collaboration with remote team members, real-time data updates, and disaster recovery planning.

Expanding Service Offerings

Diversify your service offerings to meet evolving client needs and maximize revenue opportunities:

1. Advisory Services: Expand beyond traditional tax preparation to offer advisory services, financial planning, and tax strategy consultations. Position yourself as a trusted advisor who provides strategic insights to optimize clients' financial outcomes.

2. Specialized Tax Services: Develop expertise in specialized tax areas (e.g., international taxation, estate planning, IRS dispute resolution) to serve niche markets and high-value clients with complex tax needs. Invest in training, certifications, and partnerships to enhance credibility and expertise.

3. Year-Round Engagement: Offer year-round services such as tax planning, quarterly reviews, and financial forecasting to maintain ongoing client engagement beyond tax season. Provide proactive advice and timely updates to help clients achieve their financial goals.

Building Strategic Partnerships

Collaborate with strategic partners to expand your reach, enhance service offerings, and unlock new growth opportunities:

1. Referral Networks: Establish referral partnerships with complementary professionals (e.g., financial advisors, attorneys, business consultants) who serve similar client demographics. Exchange referrals, co-host workshops, and share resources to mutually benefit from client referrals.

2. Industry Collaborations: Participate in industry associations, local chambers of commerce, and networking groups to build relationships with fellow professionals and potential clients. Contribute expertise through speaking engagements, webinars, and thought leadership articles to showcase your knowledge and credibility.

3. Technology Integration: Partner with technology providers, software developers, or fintech startups to integrate innovative solutions into your service offerings. Collaborate on product development, beta testing, or pilot programs to leverage emerging technologies that enhance client value and operational efficiency.

Measuring and Optimizing Growth

Monitor key performance indicators (KPIs) to track progress, measure success, and optimize growth strategies:

1. Performance Metrics: Define measurable goals and KPIs (e.g., client acquisition cost, revenue per client, client retention rate) to evaluate the effectiveness of growth initiatives. Analyze data regularly to identify trends, assess ROI, and make data-driven decisions.

2. Client Feedback: Solicit feedback from clients through satisfaction surveys, testimonials, and post-service evaluations. Use client insights to refine service offerings, improve customer experience, and address areas for enhancement.

3. Continuous Improvement: Embrace a culture of continuous improvement by seeking employee feedback, investing in staff training, and adapting strategies based on market feedback and industry trends. Stay agile, responsive to client needs, and proactive in anticipating market changes.

Conclusion

Growing your tax preparation business requires strategic planning, innovation, and a client-centric approach to service delivery. By assessing your current position, developing a growth strategy, leveraging technology, expanding service offerings, building strategic partnerships, and measuring progress, you can achieve sustainable growth and differentiation in a competitive market. Focus on delivering exceptional value, fostering client relationships, and adapting to industry dynamics to position your business for long-term success and profitability. With dedication, creativity, and a commitment to excellence, you're well-positioned to expand your reach, enhance service capabilities, and achieve your growth objectives in the evolving tax preparation landscape.

Chapter 12: Marketing Your Tax Preparation Business

Welcome to the chapter dedicated to marketing strategies for your tax preparation business! Effective marketing is essential for attracting new clients, increasing brand awareness, and positioning your business as a trusted advisor in the competitive tax services industry. This chapter explores proven marketing techniques, digital strategies, and promotional tactics to enhance visibility, drive client acquisition, and foster business growth.

Understanding Your Target Audience

Before diving into marketing strategies, it's crucial to understand your target audience—the individuals and businesses who are most likely to benefit from your tax preparation services:

1. Demographic Analysis: Identify key demographic factors such as age, income level, occupation, and geographic location that define your ideal clients. Tailor your marketing messages and outreach efforts to resonate with the specific needs and preferences of your target audience.

2. Client Personas: Create client personas or profiles that represent typical clients within your target market segments. Consider their goals, challenges, motivations, and decision-making criteria when crafting marketing campaigns and messaging.

3. Client Segmentation: Segment your client base into distinct groups based on common characteristics or behaviors. Develop targeted marketing strategies for each segment to maximize relevance and engagement with tailored content and offers.

Developing a Marketing Strategy

Craft a comprehensive marketing strategy that aligns with your business goals, differentiates your brand, and attracts potential clients:

1. Brand Positioning: Define your unique selling proposition (USP) and brand identity that sets your tax preparation services apart from competitors. Communicate your expertise, reliability, and commitment to client satisfaction through compelling brand messaging.

2. Marketing Channels: Select effective marketing channels to reach and engage your target audience. Consider a mix of digital marketing (e.g., website, social media, email marketing), traditional advertising (e.g., print ads, direct mail), networking events, and community outreach initiatives.

3. Content Marketing: Create valuable and informative content that educates, empowers, and resonates with your target audience. Develop blog posts, articles, whitepapers, and infographics that address common tax-related questions, offer tips for tax planning, or highlight industry insights.

Digital Marketing Strategies

Harness the power of digital marketing to expand your online presence, attract leads, and convert prospects into clients:

1. Professional Website: Maintain a user-friendly website that serves as a central hub for your tax preparation services. Optimize your website for search engines (SEO) to improve visibility in organic search results and attract qualified traffic.

2. Search Engine Optimization (SEO): Implement SEO best practices to enhance your website's ranking on search engine results pages (SERPs). Use relevant keywords, meta descriptions, alt text for images, and internal linking to improve search engine visibility and attract organic traffic.

3. Pay-Per-Click Advertising (PPC): Launch targeted PPC campaigns on search engines (e.g., Google Ads) and social media platforms (e.g., Facebook Ads) to drive immediate traffic to your website. Set specific targeting criteria, monitor campaign performance, and optimize ad spend to maximize ROI.

Building Online Presence and Reputation

Establish a strong online presence and cultivate a positive reputation to build trust and credibility with potential clients:

1. Social Media Marketing: Leverage social media platforms (e.g., LinkedIn, Twitter, Facebook, Instagram) to share valuable content, engage with followers, and showcase your expertise in tax preparation. Participate in industry discussions, join relevant groups, and share client testimonials to build credibility.

2. Online Reviews and Testimonials: Encourage satisfied clients to leave reviews and testimonials on your website, Google My Business, Yelp, and industry-specific review platforms. Positive reviews enhance your online reputation and influence potential clients' decision-making.

3. Thought Leadership: Establish yourself as a thought leader in tax preparation by publishing articles, guest blogs, or participating in podcasts/webinars. Share insights, industry trends, and expert commentary to demonstrate your knowledge and attract followers who value your expertise.

Client Referral Programs

Harness the power of client referrals to expand your client base through word-of-mouth marketing:

1. Referral Incentives: Offer incentives or rewards (e.g., discounts on future services, gift cards) to clients who refer new business to your tax preparation services. Promote referral programs through email newsletters, social media posts, and client communications.

2. Networking and Partnerships: Cultivate relationships with complementary professionals (e.g., financial advisors, attorneys, small business consultants) who can refer clients in need of tax preparation services. Attend networking events, join industry associations, and participate in local business communities to expand your referral network.

3. Client Appreciation Events: Host client appreciation events, workshops, or webinars to foster relationships, educate clients on tax-related topics, and encourage referrals. Provide valuable insights, networking opportunities, and personalized interactions to enhance client loyalty and referral generation.

Measuring Marketing Effectiveness

Monitor and evaluate the performance of your marketing efforts to optimize strategies and achieve measurable results:

1. Key Performance Indicators (KPIs): Track KPIs such as website traffic, lead conversion rates, client acquisition cost (CAC), and return on investment (ROI) for marketing campaigns. Use analytics tools (e.g., Google Analytics, social media insights) to gain actionable insights and make data-driven decisions.

2. A/B Testing: Conduct A/B testing (split testing) on marketing campaigns, landing pages, and email subject lines to optimize performance and identify strategies that resonate most with your target audience. Test variables such as headlines, visuals, calls-to-action (CTAs), and messaging to improve engagement and conversion rates.

3. Client Feedback and Surveys: Solicit feedback from clients through satisfaction surveys, post-service evaluations, and client interviews. Use insights to refine marketing messages, improve service delivery, and address areas for enhancement to better meet client expectations.

Conclusion

Marketing your tax preparation business effectively requires a strategic approach, creativity, and a deep understanding of your target audience. By defining your brand, leveraging digital marketing channels, building a strong online presence, nurturing client relationships, and measuring marketing effectiveness, you can attract new clients, increase visibility, and achieve sustainable growth. Embrace innovation, adapt to evolving market trends, and continuously refine your marketing strategies to differentiate your business and position yourself as a trusted advisor in the competitive tax services industry.

Chapter 13: Client Retention Strategies for Your Tax Preparation Business

Welcome to the chapter focused on client retention strategies for your tax preparation business! Retaining existing clients is essential for long-term success, profitability, and sustainable growth. This chapter explores effective retention strategies, relationship-building techniques, and proactive approaches to enhance client satisfaction, loyalty, and advocacy.

Understanding the Importance of Client Retention

Client retention is more than retaining business; it's about nurturing relationships, delivering exceptional service, and demonstrating value consistently. Here's why client retention matters:

1. Revenue Stability: Retaining clients reduces reliance on new client acquisition and stabilizes revenue streams throughout the year, beyond tax season peaks.

2. Cost Efficiency: It costs less to retain existing clients than to acquire new ones. Building long-term relationships minimizes marketing and sales expenses associated with client acquisition.

3. Referral Potential: Satisfied clients are more likely to refer friends, family, and colleagues to your tax preparation services, expanding your client base through word-of-mouth referrals.

Developing a Client-Centric Culture

Foster a client-centric culture within your tax preparation business to prioritize client satisfaction and exceed expectations:

1. Personalized Service: Tailor your services to meet each client's unique needs, preferences, and financial goals. Offer personalized tax planning advice, proactive communication, and customized solutions that demonstrate your commitment to client success.

2. Responsive Communication: Maintain open lines of communication with clients through multiple channels (e.g., phone, email, client portals). Respond promptly to inquiries, provide timely updates on tax filings, and address client concerns with empathy and professionalism.

3. Relationship Building: Build rapport and trust with clients by establishing genuine connections and understanding their individual circumstances. Engage in active listening, ask thoughtful questions, and show empathy to strengthen client relationships over time.

Delivering Exceptional Service

Consistently deliver high-quality service experiences that exceed client expectations and differentiate your tax preparation business:

1. Service Excellence: Strive for excellence in every client interaction, from initial consultation to tax filing and beyond. Anticipate client needs, deliver accurate tax advice, and provide proactive recommendations to optimize financial outcomes.

2. Accessibility and Convenience: Offer flexible scheduling options, online appointment booking, and virtual consultation services to accommodate clients' busy schedules and preferences. Embrace technology to enhance accessibility and streamline communication.

3. Transparent Pricing: Communicate transparently about pricing, fees, and billing practices upfront to prevent misunderstandings and build trust. Provide clear estimates, discuss service expectations, and outline the value clients receive from your tax preparation services.

Proactive Client Engagement

Engage clients proactively throughout the year to maintain ongoing relationships and reinforce your value as a trusted advisor:

1. Year-Round Communication: Stay connected with clients beyond tax season by offering year-round services such as tax planning, financial reviews, and regulatory updates. Send newsletters, informative articles, and personalized tax tips to keep clients informed and engaged.

2. Educational Workshops: Host educational workshops, webinars, or seminars on tax-related topics of interest to clients. Share insights, best practices, and industry trends to empower clients with knowledge and demonstrate your expertise as a tax professional.

3. Client Appreciation Events: Show appreciation for client loyalty by organizing client appreciation events, social gatherings, or networking opportunities. Celebrate milestones, recognize client achievements, and foster a sense of community among your client base.

Implementing Client Feedback Mechanisms

Gather client feedback regularly to assess satisfaction levels, identify areas for improvement, and strengthen service delivery:

1. Client Surveys: Conduct client satisfaction surveys periodically to gather feedback on service experiences, communication effectiveness, and overall satisfaction with your tax preparation services. Use survey insights to address client concerns and enhance service quality.

2. Feedback Loops: Establish feedback loops to capture real-time client feedback throughout the tax preparation process. Encourage clients to share suggestions, voice concerns, and provide testimonials that contribute to continuous improvement initiatives.

3. Actionable Insights: Analyze client feedback data to identify trends, patterns, and actionable insights for enhancing client retention strategies. Implement feedback-driven improvements, address service gaps, and prioritize initiatives that align with client preferences and expectations.

Building Client Loyalty and Advocacy

Cultivate client loyalty and advocacy through exceptional service delivery, proactive engagement, and personalized client experiences:

1. Loyalty Programs: Reward client loyalty with exclusive benefits, incentives, or loyalty programs that recognize repeat business and referrals. Offer discounts on future services, referral bonuses, or VIP treatment to incentivize ongoing engagement and client retention.

2. Client Testimonials and Referrals: Encourage satisfied clients to provide testimonials, reviews, and referrals that endorse your tax preparation services. Showcase client success stories, testimonials, and case studies on your website, social media, and marketing materials to build credibility and attract new clients.

3. Relationship Management: Invest in relationship management strategies that prioritize long-term client relationships and foster mutual trust. Maintain regular contact, express gratitude for client loyalty, and demonstrate your commitment to their financial well-being and success.

Conclusion

Client retention is integral to the sustained growth and success of your tax preparation business. By prioritizing client-centricity, delivering exceptional service experiences, fostering proactive client engagement, implementing feedback mechanisms, and cultivating client loyalty and advocacy, you can strengthen relationships, enhance satisfaction, and differentiate your business in a competitive marketplace. Embrace a commitment to continuous improvement, adapt to client preferences, and strive to exceed expectations to build lasting client relationships that drive business growth and prosperity.

Chapter 14: Managing Finances and Cash Flow in Your Tax Preparation Business

Welcome to the chapter dedicated to managing finances and cash flow in your tax preparation business! Effectively managing finances is essential for sustaining operations, achieving profitability, and maintaining financial health throughout the year. This chapter explores practical strategies, financial management principles, and proactive approaches to optimize cash flow, monitor expenses, and ensure financial stability.

Understanding Financial Management

Financial management involves overseeing your tax preparation business's financial resources, budgeting, and strategic decision-making to achieve business objectives:

1. Budgeting and Forecasting: Develop a comprehensive budget that outlines projected revenues, expenses, and financial goals for the fiscal year. Forecast cash flow, anticipate seasonal fluctuations, and allocate resources strategically to align with business growth initiatives.

2. Expense Management: Monitor and control operating expenses, overhead costs, and discretionary spending to optimize financial resources and improve profitability margins. Implement cost-saving measures, negotiate vendor contracts, and prioritize investments that yield long-term returns.

3. Financial Reporting: Generate regular financial reports (e.g., profit and loss statements, balance sheets, cash flow statements) to assess business performance, track financial trends, and make informed decisions. Use financial data to identify areas for improvement, measure profitability, and allocate resources effectively.

Cash Flow Management Strategies

Manage cash flow effectively to maintain liquidity, meet financial obligations, and support day-to-day operations in your tax preparation business:

1. Cash Flow Forecasting: Forecast cash inflows and outflows based on historical data, client billing cycles, and seasonal demand fluctuations. Anticipate cash flow gaps, plan for contingencies, and maintain adequate cash reserves to cover operational expenses.

2. Accounts Receivable Management: Implement policies and procedures to accelerate accounts receivable collections and minimize overdue payments. Issue invoices promptly, offer multiple payment options (e.g., online payments, credit cards), and follow up with clients on outstanding balances to improve cash flow.

3. Accounts Payable Strategies: Negotiate favorable payment terms with vendors, suppliers, and service providers to optimize cash flow management. Prioritize payments based on due dates, negotiate early payment discounts, and monitor accounts payable aging to avoid late fees or penalties.

Financial Planning and Investment

Develop a strategic financial plan that aligns with business goals, mitigates risks, and supports long-term growth:

1. Capital Expenditure Planning: Evaluate capital investment opportunities (e.g., technology upgrades, office renovations) that enhance operational efficiency, client service delivery, and competitive advantage. Prioritize investments that yield significant returns and align with business expansion objectives.

2. Emergency Fund and Reserves: Establish an emergency fund or financial reserves to buffer against unforeseen expenses, economic downturns, or disruptions in cash flow. Maintain liquid assets and contingency plans to mitigate financial risks and sustain business operations during challenging times.

3. Debt Management: Manage business debt responsibly by monitoring interest rates, repayment schedules, and debt-to-equity ratios. Refinance high-interest loans, consolidate debt where feasible, and prioritize debt repayment to reduce financial liabilities and improve cash flow liquidity.

Tax Planning and Compliance

Ensure compliance with tax obligations and leverage tax planning strategies to optimize financial outcomes:

1. Tax Efficiency: Work with a qualified tax advisor or accountant to implement tax planning strategies that minimize tax liabilities, maximize deductions, and optimize tax credits available to your tax preparation business. Stay informed about changes in tax laws, regulations, and filing deadlines to avoid penalties or audits.

2. Quarterly Tax Payments: Make timely quarterly tax payments to federal, state, and local tax authorities based on estimated income and self-employment taxes. Plan ahead for tax obligations, maintain accurate records, and consult with tax professionals to ensure compliance and avoid tax-related issues.

3. Financial Compliance: Adhere to regulatory requirements, licensing obligations, and industry standards governing financial practices in the tax preparation industry. Maintain accurate financial records, cooperate with audits or regulatory inspections, and uphold ethical standards in financial reporting and transparency.

Risk Management and Insurance

Mitigate business risks through comprehensive risk management strategies and insurance coverage:

1. Risk Assessment: Conduct a risk assessment to identify potential threats to business continuity, financial stability, or operational integrity. Develop risk mitigation strategies, implement internal controls, and monitor external factors that impact business operations.

2. Business Insurance: Obtain appropriate insurance coverage (e.g., professional liability insurance, general liability insurance, cybersecurity insurance) to protect against legal claims, client disputes, data breaches, or unforeseen events that may disrupt business operations or financial stability.

3. Contingency Planning: Develop a contingency plan outlining procedures and protocols for managing emergencies, business disruptions, or unexpected financial challenges. Maintain business continuity strategies, backup systems, and disaster recovery plans to minimize downtime and mitigate financial losses.

Conclusion

Effective financial management is critical to the success and sustainability of your tax preparation business. By implementing sound financial practices, managing cash flow effectively, planning for financial contingencies, and prioritizing tax compliance, you can optimize profitability, mitigate risks, and achieve long-term financial health. Embrace financial planning as a strategic tool to support business growth, make informed decisions, and navigate economic uncertainties with confidence. With diligence, foresight, and a commitment to financial excellence, you can position your tax preparation business for financial success and resilience in a competitive marketplace.

Chapter 15: Scaling Your Tax Preparation Business

Welcome to the chapter focused on scaling your tax preparation business! Scaling involves expanding operations, increasing revenue streams, and enhancing organizational capacity to accommodate growth. This chapter explores strategic growth initiatives, operational scalability, team expansion, and managerial considerations to successfully scale your tax preparation business.

Assessing Readiness for Growth

Before embarking on scaling initiatives, assess your business's current readiness and identify opportunities for expansion:

1. **Market Demand:** Evaluate market demand for tax preparation services in your target demographics, industries, and geographic regions. Identify growth opportunities, emerging trends, and niche markets where demand for specialized tax expertise is high.

2. **Operational Efficiency:** Review existing workflows, operational processes, and technology infrastructure to identify areas for improvement and scalability. Streamline workflows, automate routine tasks, and leverage technology solutions to enhance efficiency and productivity.

3. **Financial Stability:** Assess financial health, profitability margins, and cash flow management practices to support business expansion. Ensure adequate funding sources, capital reserves, and financial resources to fund scaling initiatives, investments in growth, and operational expansion.

Developing a Scalability Strategy

Craft a scalability strategy that aligns with business objectives, market opportunities, and long-term growth aspirations:

1. **Business Model Evaluation:** Evaluate your current business model and revenue streams. Consider diversifying service offerings, introducing new products or packages, or exploring recurring revenue models (e.g., subscription-based services) to enhance scalability and revenue predictability.

2. **Geographic Expansion:** Explore opportunities for geographic expansion into new markets or regions where demand for tax preparation services is growing. Conduct market research, assess competitive landscapes, and adapt service offerings to meet local market needs and preferences.

3. Strategic Partnerships: Form strategic partnerships with complementary businesses (e.g., financial advisors, small business consultants) to expand service capabilities, cross-sell services, and leverage shared resources for mutual growth and client acquisition.

Leveraging Technology and Innovation

Harness technology and innovation to streamline operations, enhance service delivery, and support business scalability:

1. Advanced Tax Preparation Software: Upgrade to advanced tax preparation software with integrated features for data management, client collaboration, and regulatory compliance. Leverage AI-powered tools, cloud-based solutions, and automation to optimize efficiency and accuracy in tax preparation processes.

2. Client Relationship Management (CRM): Implement a CRM system to manage client interactions, track leads, and nurture relationships throughout the client lifecycle. Utilize CRM data analytics, personalized communication tools, and client feedback mechanisms to enhance client engagement and retention.

3. Scalable Infrastructure: Invest in scalable infrastructure, IT systems, and digital platforms that support business growth and accommodate increasing client volumes. Ensure scalability in data storage, network bandwidth, and cybersecurity measures to maintain operational resilience and data security.

Building a High-Performance Team

Expand your team strategically to support business growth, enhance service delivery, and maintain high standards of client satisfaction:

1. Talent Acquisition: Recruit skilled tax professionals, certified public accountants (CPAs), and financial advisors with expertise in tax preparation, regulatory compliance, and client service excellence. Prioritize cultural fit, professional qualifications, and commitment to ongoing learning and development.

2. Training and Development: Invest in training programs, professional certifications, and continuing education opportunities to equip team members with updated tax knowledge, industry best practices, and technical skills. Foster a culture of learning, mentorship, and career advancement to retain top talent and promote organizational growth.

3. Team Collaboration: Promote cross-functional collaboration, knowledge sharing, and teamwork among team members to optimize service delivery, streamline workflows, and foster innovation. Establish clear roles, responsibilities, and performance metrics to align team efforts with business objectives and client expectations.

Strategic Marketing and Client Acquisition

Expand your client base and increase market penetration through targeted marketing initiatives and client acquisition strategies:

1. Digital Marketing Campaigns: Launch targeted digital marketing campaigns (e.g., SEO, PPC advertising, social media marketing) to enhance online visibility, attract qualified leads, and generate client inquiries. Develop compelling content, educational resources, and thought leadership content to position your business as a trusted authority in tax preparation.

2. Referral Programs: Implement referral programs, incentives, and client loyalty initiatives to encourage existing clients, strategic partners, and professional networks to refer new business. Reward referrals with incentives, discounts, or exclusive benefits to incentivize client advocacy and expand your client base through word-of-mouth marketing.

3. Thought Leadership and Networking: Establish thought leadership through speaking engagements, webinars, industry publications, and networking events. Share insights, industry trends, and expert commentary to build credibility, expand professional networks, and attract prospective clients seeking specialized tax expertise.

Measuring Success and Continuous Improvement

Monitor key performance indicators (KPIs), evaluate scalability initiatives, and adapt strategies for continuous improvement and business growth:

1. Performance Metrics: Track KPIs such as client acquisition cost (CAC), revenue growth, client retention rate, and profitability margins to measure the effectiveness of scaling initiatives. Analyze data insights, identify trends, and make data-driven decisions to optimize operational efficiency and financial performance.

2. Client Feedback and Satisfaction: Solicit client feedback through satisfaction surveys, testimonials, and post-service evaluations to assess service quality, identify areas for enhancement, and prioritize client-centric improvements. Use client insights to refine service offerings, enhance client experience, and strengthen client relationships.

3. Agility and Adaptability: Maintain agility and adaptability in response to market dynamics, regulatory changes, and industry trends. Anticipate evolving client needs, innovate proactively, and pivot strategies as needed to capitalize on emerging opportunities and sustain competitive advantage in the tax preparation industry.

Conclusion

Scaling your tax preparation business requires strategic planning, operational scalability, technology adoption, talent acquisition, and client-centric growth strategies. By developing a scalability strategy aligned with business objectives, leveraging technology and innovation, building a high-performance team, implementing strategic marketing initiatives, and measuring success through KPIs and client feedback, you can achieve sustainable growth, expand market presence, and enhance profitability. Embrace a culture of innovation, continuous improvement, and client-centricity to navigate challenges, capitalize on growth opportunities, and position your tax preparation business for long-term success in a competitive marketplace.

Chapter 16: Adapting to Change in Your Tax Preparation Business

Welcome to the chapter dedicated to adapting to change in your tax preparation business! In today's dynamic business environment, adaptability is key to maintaining relevance, driving innovation, and sustaining long-term success. This chapter explores strategies, best practices, and proactive approaches to navigate change effectively, capitalize on opportunities, and overcome challenges in the tax preparation industry.

Embracing a Culture of Adaptability

Cultivate a culture of adaptability within your tax preparation business to foster resilience, creativity, and continuous improvement:

1. Mindset Shift: Embrace change as an opportunity for growth, learning, and innovation rather than a barrier or disruption. Foster a mindset of curiosity, flexibility, and proactive problem-solving among team members to navigate uncertainties and capitalize on new opportunities.

2. Open Communication: Encourage open communication, transparency, and collaboration across all levels of your organization. Solicit feedback, ideas, and suggestions from team members, clients, and stakeholders to harness collective insights and drive informed decision-making.

3. Agility and Flexibility: Build agility and flexibility into operational processes, workflows, and decision-making frameworks. Adapt quickly to market shifts, regulatory changes, and client needs by adjusting strategies, reallocating resources, and seizing emerging opportunities proactively.

Monitoring Industry Trends and Market Dynamics

Stay informed about industry trends, market developments, and regulatory changes that impact the tax preparation landscape:

1. Industry Research: Conduct ongoing research, monitor industry publications, and participate in professional associations to stay abreast of evolving tax laws, compliance requirements, and industry best practices. Stay informed about technological advancements, competitive trends, and emerging opportunities that shape the future of tax services.

2. Client Insights: Listen to client feedback, anticipate evolving client needs, and adapt service offerings accordingly. Conduct client surveys, gather testimonials, and analyze client data to identify trends, preferences, and opportunities for service enhancement or innovation.

3. Competitive Analysis: Perform competitive analysis to benchmark against industry peers, identify competitive advantages, and differentiate your tax preparation services. Evaluate competitor strategies, pricing models, and service offerings to refine your value proposition and position your business strategically in the marketplace.

Leveraging Technology and Innovation

Harness technology and innovation to drive operational efficiency, enhance service delivery, and differentiate your tax preparation business:

1. Advanced Tax Software: Invest in advanced tax preparation software with integrated features for data management, client collaboration, and regulatory compliance. Leverage AI-powered tools, machine learning algorithms, and cloud-based solutions to automate routine tasks, streamline workflows, and improve accuracy in tax filings.

2. Client-Centric Technology: Adopt client portals, digital communication tools, and secure online platforms to enhance client interactions, streamline document exchange, and facilitate remote collaboration. Offer virtual consultation services, online appointment scheduling, and personalized client experiences to accommodate changing client preferences.

3. Cybersecurity Measures: Implement robust cybersecurity measures, data encryption protocols, and privacy safeguards to protect sensitive client information, comply with data protection regulations, and mitigate cybersecurity risks. Stay vigilant against cyber threats, educate team members about security best practices, and prioritize data integrity and confidentiality.

Agile Decision-Making and Strategic Planning

Embrace agile decision-making processes and strategic planning frameworks to navigate change effectively and capitalize on opportunities:

1. Scenario Planning: Develop contingency plans and scenario analysis to anticipate potential disruptions, economic uncertainties, or regulatory changes. Evaluate alternative strategies, risk mitigation measures, and business continuity plans to maintain operational resilience and adaptability.

2. Strategic Partnerships: Form strategic alliances, partnerships, or collaborations with complementary businesses, industry experts, or technology providers to expand service capabilities, access new markets, and leverage shared resources for mutual growth. Foster collaborative relationships that foster innovation, mutual support, and strategic alignment.

3. Change Management: Implement structured change management processes, communication strategies, and training programs to facilitate organizational change, minimize resistance, and empower team members to embrace new initiatives or operational improvements. Provide leadership support, resources, and incentives to promote a culture of change readiness and continuous improvement.

Resilience and Adaptation in Challenging Times

Build resilience, adaptability, and proactive resilience to navigate economic downturns, market fluctuations, or unforeseen challenges:

1. Financial Preparedness: Maintain financial stability, liquidity, and cash flow management practices to withstand economic uncertainties or disruptions. Establish contingency funds, monitor financial health indicators, and implement cost-saving measures to preserve profitability and sustain business operations.

2. Client-Centric Focus: Prioritize client relationships, responsiveness, and service excellence during challenging times. Offer personalized support, financial guidance, and proactive communication to reassure clients, address concerns, and maintain trust in your tax preparation services.

3. Continuous Learning and Development: Invest in ongoing learning initiatives, professional development programs, and skill enhancement opportunities for team members. Encourage continuous learning, adaptability to technological advancements, and industry trends to stay ahead of competition and deliver value-added services to clients.

Conclusion

Adapting to change is essential for the growth, resilience, and sustainability of your tax preparation business. By embracing a culture of adaptability, monitoring industry trends, leveraging technology and innovation, practicing agile decision-making, and fostering resilience during challenging times, you can navigate uncertainties, capitalize on opportunities, and position your business for long-term success in the evolving tax services industry. Embrace change as a catalyst for innovation, growth, and strategic advancement to maintain competitive advantage and achieve business excellence in a dynamic marketplace.

Chapter 17: Marketing Strategies for Your Tax Preparation Business

Welcome to the chapter dedicated to marketing strategies for your tax preparation business! Effective marketing plays a crucial role in attracting clients, building brand visibility, and differentiating your services in a competitive marketplace. This chapter explores proven marketing tactics, digital strategies, client acquisition techniques, and branding essentials tailored for tax preparation professionals.

Understanding Your Target Audience

Identifying and understanding your target audience is the foundation of successful marketing strategies:

1. Demographic Segmentation: Define your ideal client demographics, including age, income level, occupation, and location. Tailor marketing messages, service offerings, and promotional campaigns to resonate with your target audience's preferences and needs.

2. Psychographic Insights: Consider psychographic factors such as lifestyle preferences, financial goals, and behavioral patterns. Understand client motivations, decision-making processes, and pain points related to tax preparation services to customize marketing approaches effectively.

3. Client Personas: Develop client personas or profiles that represent different segments of your target audience. Use personas to create targeted marketing campaigns, craft compelling messaging, and align service delivery with client expectations and preferences.

Building a Strong Brand Identity

Establish a distinctive brand identity that communicates professionalism, trustworthiness, and expertise in tax preparation:

1. Brand Messaging: Define your unique value proposition, brand promise, and core messaging points that differentiate your tax preparation services from competitors. Communicate your expertise, industry specialization, and commitment to client satisfaction through consistent messaging.

2. Visual Branding: Design a cohesive visual identity, including a logo, color palette, typography, and brand imagery that reflects your brand personality and resonates with your target audience. Ensure visual consistency across marketing materials, website, social media profiles, and client communications.

3. Brand Voice: Develop a consistent brand voice and tone that reflects your business values, client-centric approach, and professional demeanor. Tailor communication styles to engage with clients authentically, convey expertise, and build trust through clear, concise, and empathetic language.

Digital Marketing Strategies

Utilize digital marketing channels and online platforms to enhance brand visibility, attract qualified leads, and engage with prospective clients:

1. Website Optimization: Create a professional, user-friendly website optimized for search engines (SEO). Incorporate relevant keywords, informative content, intuitive navigation, and mobile responsiveness to improve online visibility and attract organic traffic.

2. Content Marketing: Develop valuable content such as blog posts, articles, infographics, and educational resources that address client questions, industry trends, and tax-related topics. Position your business as a thought leader, provide insights, and establish credibility to attract and engage prospective clients.

3. Social Media Presence: Establish a presence on social media platforms (e.g., LinkedIn, Facebook, Twitter) to connect with clients, industry professionals, and potential referral partners. Share informative content, client testimonials, industry updates, and engage in conversations to build relationships and expand your online network.

Client Acquisition and Lead Generation

Implement targeted client acquisition strategies to attract new clients and expand your customer base:

1. Referral Programs: Develop referral programs, incentives, and client loyalty initiatives to encourage satisfied clients, business partners, and professional networks to refer new clients. Reward referrals with discounts, exclusive offers, or incentives to incentivize word-of-mouth marketing and client advocacy.

2. Networking and Partnerships: Attend industry events, networking functions, and community gatherings to build relationships with local businesses, chambers of commerce, and professional associations. Cultivate partnerships, collaborate on joint marketing initiatives, and leverage referral networks to generate qualified leads and client referrals.

3. Online Advertising: Launch targeted online advertising campaigns (e.g., Google Ads, social media ads) to reach specific demographics, geographic areas, or client segments seeking tax preparation services. Optimize ad campaigns, track performance metrics, and adjust strategies based on analytics to maximize return on investment (ROI).

Client Engagement and Relationship Management

Nurture client relationships, enhance satisfaction, and promote loyalty through effective client engagement strategies:

1. Personalized Communication: Maintain regular communication with clients through personalized emails, newsletters, and updates on tax-related news, deadlines, and industry insights. Tailor communications to address individual client needs, preferences, and financial goals effectively.

2. Client Education: Offer educational workshops, webinars, or seminars on tax planning strategies, financial literacy topics, and regulatory updates. Empower clients with knowledge, resources, and actionable insights to make informed decisions and optimize their financial outcomes.

3. Feedback and Satisfaction Surveys: Solicit client feedback through satisfaction surveys, post-service evaluations, and testimonials to gauge satisfaction levels, identify areas for improvement, and enhance service quality. Use client insights to refine service offerings, address concerns proactively, and strengthen client relationships.

Measuring Marketing Effectiveness

Monitor key performance indicators (KPIs) and metrics to assess the effectiveness of your marketing strategies and campaign outcomes:

1. Lead Conversion Rate: Track the percentage of leads generated through marketing efforts that convert into paying clients. Analyze conversion rates by marketing channel, campaign type, and client acquisition source to optimize lead generation strategies and improve conversion efficiency.

2. Return on Investment (ROI): Calculate the ROI of marketing campaigns by comparing the cost of marketing initiatives to the revenue generated from acquired clients. Evaluate campaign performance, cost-effectiveness, and profitability to allocate marketing budgets strategically and prioritize high-performing channels.

3. Client Retention Rate: Measure client retention rates and assess client churn rates to evaluate the effectiveness of client engagement strategies, satisfaction levels, and loyalty initiatives. Implement retention strategies, personalized follow-up, and ongoing client communication to foster long-term client relationships and reduce attrition.

Conclusion

Effective marketing strategies are essential for attracting clients, building brand visibility, and achieving business growth in the competitive tax preparation industry. By understanding your target audience, developing a strong brand identity, leveraging digital marketing channels, implementing client acquisition strategies, nurturing client relationships, and measuring marketing effectiveness, you can enhance market presence, generate qualified leads, and position your tax preparation business for long-term success. Embrace innovation, adapt to evolving client needs, and prioritize client-centricity to differentiate your services, drive business growth, and achieve marketing excellence in the dynamic landscape of tax services.

Chapter 18: Client Relationship Management for Your Tax Preparation Business

Welcome to the chapter dedicated to client relationship management (CRM) for your tax preparation business! Building strong client relationships is essential for client satisfaction, retention, and business growth. This chapter explores strategies, best practices, and effective approaches to cultivate positive client experiences, foster loyalty, and enhance long-term relationships in the tax preparation industry.

Importance of Client Relationship Management

Client relationship management is more than just managing interactions; it's about understanding client needs, exceeding expectations, and delivering exceptional service:

1. Client-Centric Approach: Adopt a client-centric mindset focused on understanding client goals, financial aspirations, and tax-related concerns. Tailor services, communication, and solutions to meet individual client needs and build trust through personalized attention.

2. Long-Term Relationships: Nurture long-term relationships built on transparency, integrity, and reliability. Prioritize client satisfaction, responsiveness, and proactive communication to foster loyalty and position your business as a trusted advisor in tax preparation.

3. Business Growth: Strengthen client relationships to drive business growth through referrals, repeat business, and positive word-of-mouth recommendations. Satisfied clients are more likely to advocate for your services, expand their engagement, and contribute to sustainable business growth.

Effective Client Communication

Effective communication is the cornerstone of successful client relationships and satisfaction:

1. Clear and Timely Communication: Communicate clearly, concisely, and promptly with clients regarding tax preparation processes, deadlines, documentation requirements, and service updates. Set expectations, provide regular updates, and address client inquiries promptly to demonstrate responsiveness and professionalism.

2. Active Listening: Practice active listening to understand client concerns, preferences, and financial goals. Validate client perspectives, ask clarifying questions, and empathize with their needs to build rapport, trust, and mutual understanding in client interactions.

3. Educational Outreach: Educate clients on tax planning strategies, regulatory changes, and financial literacy topics through informative workshops, webinars, or personalized consultations. Empower clients with knowledge, resources, and actionable insights to make informed decisions and achieve their financial objectives.

Personalized Client Service

Deliver personalized client service experiences that prioritize individualized attention and exceed client expectations:

1. Customized Solutions: Tailor tax preparation services to address client-specific circumstances, financial objectives, and tax compliance requirements. Offer personalized recommendations, strategic advice, and proactive solutions that optimize tax efficiency and maximize financial outcomes for clients.

2. Relationship Building: Build rapport and trust through personalized interactions, remembering client preferences, milestones, and important dates. Celebrate client achievements, acknowledge milestones (e.g., anniversaries, business expansions), and demonstrate appreciation for their loyalty and partnership.

3. Client Feedback: Solicit client feedback through satisfaction surveys, post-service evaluations, and testimonials to gauge client satisfaction levels and identify areas for improvement. Use client insights to refine service offerings, enhance service delivery, and address client concerns proactively.

Leveraging Technology in CRM

Utilize CRM software and digital tools to streamline client management, enhance service delivery, and maintain client relationships:

1. CRM Systems: Implement a CRM system to centralize client data, track interactions, and manage client relationships efficiently. Use CRM analytics, client segmentation, and personalized communication tools to tailor marketing campaigns, nurture leads, and strengthen client engagement.

2. Client Portals: Offer secure client portals or digital platforms for document exchange, appointment scheduling, and real-time communication. Provide clients with convenient access to tax documents, financial reports, and service updates while ensuring data security and confidentiality.

3. Automation and Efficiency: Automate routine tasks, appointment reminders, and client communications to improve operational efficiency, minimize administrative burdens, and enhance client service responsiveness. Leverage automation to streamline workflows, reduce errors, and deliver consistent service experiences.

Handling Client Challenges and Resolving Issues

Address client challenges, concerns, or disputes effectively to maintain trust, resolve issues promptly, and preserve client relationships:

1. Proactive Resolution: Anticipate potential client issues or misunderstandings by setting clear expectations, communicating policies, and providing transparent information throughout the engagement. Address client concerns promptly, offer solutions, and follow up to ensure client satisfaction and resolution.

2. Client Advocacy: Advocate on behalf of clients with tax authorities, regulatory agencies, or third parties to resolve complex issues, disputes, or compliance challenges. Demonstrate commitment to client interests, uphold ethical standards, and protect client confidentiality in all interactions.

3. Continuous Improvement: Continuously evaluate client feedback, monitor client satisfaction metrics, and implement process improvements to enhance service quality, address recurring issues, and exceed client expectations. Embrace a culture of continuous improvement, learning, and innovation to evolve client service practices and maintain competitive advantage.

Conclusion

Effective client relationship management is fundamental to the success, growth, and sustainability of your tax preparation business. By adopting a client-centric approach, prioritizing clear communication, delivering personalized service experiences, leveraging technology, and addressing client challenges proactively, you can cultivate strong client relationships, foster loyalty, and differentiate your services in the competitive tax services industry. Embrace CRM as a strategic tool to enhance client satisfaction, drive business growth, and position your tax preparation business as a trusted advisor and partner in achieving financial success for your clients.

Chapter 19: Financial Management Tips for Your Tax Preparation Business

Welcome to the chapter dedicated to financial management tips for your tax preparation business! Effective financial management is crucial for maintaining profitability, managing cash flow, and achieving long-term financial sustainability. This chapter explores key strategies, best practices, and practical tips to optimize financial health, maximize revenue, and mitigate financial risks in the tax preparation industry.

Establishing Financial Goals and Budgeting

Setting clear financial goals and implementing a structured budgeting process are essential for financial stability and business growth:

1. Goal Setting: Define short-term and long-term financial goals for your tax preparation business, such as revenue targets, profit margins, client acquisition metrics, and business expansion plans. Align financial goals with strategic objectives to prioritize resource allocation and investment decisions.

2. Budget Development: Develop a comprehensive budget that outlines anticipated revenues, operating expenses, capital investments, and contingency reserves. Monitor budget performance regularly, adjust forecasts based on business trends, and allocate resources effectively to achieve financial objectives and operational efficiency.

3. Cash Flow Management: Implement robust cash flow management practices to monitor cash inflows, outflows, and liquidity requirements. Forecast cash flow projections, maintain adequate working capital reserves, and manage receivables/payables effectively to ensure financial stability and meet financial obligations on time.

Pricing Strategies and Revenue Optimization

Develop competitive pricing strategies and revenue optimization tactics to maximize profitability and client value:

1. Pricing Strategy: Determine pricing models, fee structures, and service pricing that reflect market dynamics, competitive benchmarks, and client value perceptions. Consider value-based pricing, tiered service packages, and seasonal pricing adjustments to align pricing strategies with client expectations and industry standards.

2. Value Proposition: Communicate your unique value proposition, expertise, and service differentiation to justify pricing and demonstrate value to clients. Articulate the benefits of your tax preparation services, industry certifications, and client satisfaction guarantees to differentiate your business and attract premium clientele.

3. Upselling and Cross-Selling: Identify opportunities to upsell additional services (e.g., tax planning, financial consulting) or cross-sell complementary products (e.g., retirement planning, investment advice) to existing clients. Leverage client relationships, identify client needs, and offer personalized recommendations to increase revenue per client and enhance service value.

Cost Management and Expense Control

Implement cost management strategies and expense control measures to optimize operational efficiency and profitability:

1. Cost Analysis: Conduct regular cost analysis to identify cost-saving opportunities, reduce overhead expenses, and optimize resource utilization. Evaluate fixed costs (e.g., rent, utilities) and variable costs (e.g., staff salaries, marketing expenses) to prioritize cost-cutting initiatives and improve financial performance.

2. Vendor Negotiation: Negotiate favorable terms with suppliers, service providers, and vendors to secure competitive pricing, discounts, and contractual agreements. Consolidate purchases, explore bulk discounts, and review vendor contracts regularly to lower procurement costs and enhance cost efficiency.

3. Technology Investments: Invest in cost-effective technology solutions, software upgrades, and automation tools to streamline operations, improve productivity, and reduce administrative overhead. Leverage cloud-based platforms, digital accounting software, and IT infrastructure to optimize workflow efficiency and minimize IT maintenance costs.

Financial Reporting and Analysis

Utilize financial reporting and analysis to monitor business performance, make data-driven decisions, and support strategic planning:

1. Financial Statements: Prepare accurate financial statements (e.g., income statement, balance sheet, cash flow statement) on a regular basis to assess business profitability, liquidity, and financial health. Analyze financial metrics, key performance indicators (KPIs), and variance analysis to evaluate operational performance and financial trends.

2. Performance Metrics: Track and measure performance metrics such as client acquisition cost (CAC), revenue growth rate, profit margins, and return on investment (ROI) to evaluate the effectiveness of business strategies and marketing initiatives. Benchmark performance against industry peers and historical data to identify areas for improvement and opportunities for growth.

3. Financial Planning: Develop financial forecasts, scenario analysis, and sensitivity analysis to anticipate business risks, economic fluctuations, and industry challenges. Use financial projections to guide strategic decision-making, allocate resources effectively, and mitigate financial risks to ensure long-term business sustainability.

Compliance and Risk Management

Adhere to regulatory compliance requirements, manage financial risks, and safeguard business assets:

1. Regulatory Compliance: Stay updated on tax regulations, accounting standards, and compliance requirements relevant to the tax preparation industry. Implement internal controls, conduct regular audits, and maintain accurate records to ensure compliance with legal obligations and regulatory guidelines.

2. Risk Assessment: Identify financial risks (e.g., cash flow volatility, client defaults, cybersecurity threats) that could impact business operations and financial stability. Develop risk mitigation strategies, contingency plans, and insurance coverage to protect against unforeseen risks and minimize potential financial losses.

3. Professional Development: Invest in ongoing training, professional certifications, and continuing education for yourself and your team members to enhance financial expertise, stay abreast of industry trends, and uphold professional standards in tax preparation and financial management.

Conclusion

Effective financial management is fundamental to achieving profitability, sustainability, and growth in your tax preparation business. By establishing clear financial goals, implementing budgeting practices, optimizing pricing strategies, managing costs efficiently, leveraging financial reporting insights, and prioritizing regulatory compliance and risk management, you can enhance financial health, maximize revenue potential, and navigate business challenges with confidence. Embrace proactive financial strategies, continuous improvement, and strategic decision-making to position your tax preparation business for long-term success and leadership in the competitive marketplace.

Chapter 20: Scaling Your Tax Preparation Business for Growth

Welcome to the chapter dedicated to scaling your tax preparation business for growth! Scaling your business involves expanding operations, increasing revenue streams, and enhancing efficiency to accommodate growth opportunities and meet client demand. This chapter explores strategies, considerations, and practical steps to scale your tax preparation business effectively while maintaining quality service and sustainable business practices.

Assessing Readiness for Growth

Before embarking on scaling efforts, assess your business's readiness and strategic alignment for growth:

1. Market Analysis: Conduct a comprehensive market analysis to identify growth opportunities, competitive landscape, and client demand for tax preparation services in your target market. Evaluate market trends, client demographics, and regulatory changes to inform expansion strategies and business decisions.

2. Operational Capacity: Evaluate your current operational capacity, infrastructure, and resources to determine scalability challenges and opportunities. Assess staffing levels, technology systems, workflow efficiencies, and infrastructure requirements needed to support increased client volume and business expansion.

3. Financial Health: Review financial performance metrics, cash flow projections, and profitability indicators to assess financial readiness for growth. Analyze funding options, capital investment needs, and financial strategies to support scaling initiatives and mitigate financial risks associated with business expansion.

Developing a Scalability Strategy

Develop a scalability strategy tailored to your business objectives, client needs, and growth aspirations:

1. Service Diversification: Expand service offerings beyond traditional tax preparation to include value-added services such as tax planning, financial consulting, retirement planning, or business advisory services. Diversify revenue streams, attract high-value clients, and differentiate your business in the competitive marketplace.

2. Geographic Expansion: Explore opportunities for geographic expansion by targeting new markets, expanding service areas, or establishing satellite offices in strategic locations. Conduct feasibility studies, assess market demand, and adapt service delivery models to meet local client needs and preferences.

3. Technology Integration: Leverage technology solutions, automation tools, and digital platforms to streamline operations, enhance service delivery, and scale efficiently. Invest in scalable IT infrastructure, cloud-based systems, and cybersecurity measures to support business growth, improve productivity, and maintain data security.

Building Strategic Partnerships and Alliances

Form strategic partnerships, alliances, or collaborations to leverage shared resources, expand market reach, and enhance service capabilities:

1. Professional Networks: Establish partnerships with complementary businesses, industry professionals, or financial advisors to cross-refer clients, collaborate on joint ventures, and enhance service offerings. Build mutually beneficial relationships that foster growth, innovation, and industry leadership.

2. Referral Networks: Develop referral relationships with attorneys, real estate agents, small business associations, and community organizations to generate qualified leads and expand client acquisition channels. Implement referral programs, incentives, and networking strategies to cultivate referral partnerships and drive business growth.

3. Technology Partnerships: Partner with technology providers, software vendors, or fintech startups to integrate advanced tools, AI-driven solutions, and innovative technologies into your service offerings. Collaborate on product development, digital transformation initiatives, and tech-driven innovations to enhance service efficiency and client satisfaction.

Staffing and Talent Management

Invest in recruiting, training, and retaining skilled professionals to support business growth and maintain service excellence:

1. Talent Acquisition: Recruit qualified tax professionals, certified public accountants (CPAs), and financial advisors with specialized expertise, industry certifications, and client service skills. Align hiring practices with business expansion goals, cultural fit, and commitment to delivering exceptional client experiences.

2. Professional Development: Provide ongoing training, professional certifications, and skill development opportunities for team members to enhance technical proficiency, stay updated on tax laws, and promote career advancement. Invest in leadership development, mentorship programs, and succession planning to cultivate future leaders within your organization.

3. Performance Management: Implement performance metrics, employee feedback mechanisms, and recognition programs to motivate team members, align performance with business goals, and foster a culture of accountability, collaboration, and continuous improvement. Provide constructive feedback, career growth opportunities, and competitive compensation packages to attract and retain top talent.

Scaling Responsibly and Sustainably

Scale your tax preparation business responsibly by prioritizing sustainability, client-centricity, and operational efficiency:

1. Client Experience: Maintain a client-centric focus by delivering personalized service, responsive communication, and proactive client engagement. Prioritize client satisfaction, loyalty, and long-term relationships to sustain business growth and differentiate your services in a competitive marketplace.

2. Operational Excellence: Streamline operational workflows, optimize resource allocation, and implement scalable processes to improve efficiency, minimize costs, and maximize productivity. Embrace innovation, technology adoption, and continuous improvement to enhance service quality and operational resilience.

3. Regulatory Compliance: Stay updated on tax regulations, compliance requirements, and industry standards to uphold ethical practices, mitigate risks, and protect client interests. Implement robust internal controls, audit procedures, and governance frameworks to ensure transparency, integrity, and regulatory compliance across business operations.

Conclusion

Scaling your tax preparation business for growth requires strategic planning, operational readiness, and a commitment to excellence in client service, technology integration, talent management, and sustainable business practices. By assessing readiness, developing a scalability strategy, fostering strategic partnerships, investing in talent development, and scaling responsibly, you can capitalize on growth opportunities, expand market presence, and achieve long-term success in the competitive tax services industry. Embrace innovation, adaptability, and a client-focused approach to drive business growth, enhance operational efficiency, and maintain leadership in a dynamic marketplace.

Chapter 21: Managing Client Expectations in Your Tax Preparation Business

Welcome to the chapter dedicated to managing client expectations in your tax preparation business! Effectively managing client expectations is crucial for fostering positive client relationships, delivering quality service, and ensuring client satisfaction throughout the tax preparation process. This chapter explores strategies, best practices, and practical tips to manage client expectations proactively, communicate effectively, and provide exceptional service in the tax preparation industry.

Understanding Client Expectations

Understanding and aligning with client expectations is essential for delivering personalized service and exceeding client satisfaction:

1. Initial Consultation: Conduct thorough initial consultations to understand client needs, financial goals, and expectations regarding tax preparation services. Ask probing questions, clarify expectations, and gather relevant information to tailor service delivery and establish clear communication channels.

2. Service Scope: Define the scope of tax preparation services, deliverables, timelines, and client responsibilities upfront to manage expectations effectively. Provide transparency regarding service fees, billing practices, and any additional services or disclaimers to avoid misunderstandings and ensure agreement on service parameters.

3. Communication Preferences: Identify client communication preferences, preferred channels (e.g., email, phone calls, in-person meetings), and frequency of updates throughout the tax preparation process. Establish open lines of communication, set response expectations, and provide regular progress updates to keep clients informed and engaged.

Setting Realistic Expectations

Set realistic expectations regarding service delivery, turnaround times, and outcomes to manage client expectations proactively:

1. Service Delivery Timelines: Communicate realistic timelines for completing tax preparation tasks, filing deadlines, and expected turnaround times based on the complexity of client tax returns and regulatory requirements. Manage client expectations regarding service delivery milestones and potential delays to ensure transparency and accountability.

2. Outcome Predictability: Educate clients on potential tax outcomes, refund expectations, tax liabilities, and compliance implications based on their financial circumstances, deductions, and credits. Discuss realistic scenarios, tax planning strategies, and potential audit risks to manage expectations regarding financial outcomes and tax obligations.

3. Process Transparency: Provide clients with a clear overview of the tax preparation process, steps involved, documentation requirements, and client responsibilities. Explain the role of tax software, IRS regulations, and tax preparation guidelines to enhance client understanding and confidence in the service delivery process.

Effective Communication Strategies

Implement effective communication strategies to maintain ongoing dialogue, address client inquiries, and manage expectations proactively:

1. Active Listening: Practice active listening to understand client concerns, clarify expectations, and empathize with client perspectives throughout the tax preparation engagement. Demonstrate attentiveness, ask clarifying questions, and validate client input to build rapport and trust in client interactions.

2. Transparent Updates: Provide timely updates, progress reports, and status updates on tax preparation tasks, milestones, and documentation requirements. Keep clients informed of any changes, updates to tax laws, filing deadlines, or IRS notifications that may impact their tax returns or financial obligations.

3. Client Education: Educate clients on tax regulations, deductions, credits, and financial planning strategies through informative workshops, webinars, or personalized consultations. Empower clients with knowledge, resources, and actionable insights to make informed decisions and optimize their financial outcomes during tax season and beyond.

Managing Challenges and Client Dissatisfaction

Address client challenges, dissatisfaction, or discrepancies with proactive communication, resolution strategies, and client-centric solutions:

1. Conflict Resolution: Handle client concerns, disputes, or dissatisfaction with empathy, professionalism, and a commitment to resolving issues promptly. Listen to client feedback, acknowledge concerns, and propose solutions or alternatives to mitigate dissatisfaction and restore client confidence in service delivery.

2. Exception Handling: Manage exceptions, unexpected tax situations, or complex client cases with transparency, integrity, and expertise.

Communicate potential challenges, risks, or discrepancies early in the process, offer solutions, and seek client input to address concerns and ensure mutual agreement on next steps.

3. Continuous Improvement: Solicit client feedback through satisfaction surveys, post-service evaluations, or testimonials to assess service quality, identify improvement opportunities, and implement process enhancements. Embrace a culture of continuous improvement, client-centricity, and operational excellence to enhance service delivery and exceed client expectations consistently.

Building Long-Term Client Relationships

Cultivate long-term client relationships based on trust, reliability, and exceptional service delivery in the tax preparation industry:

1. Personalized Engagement: Foster personalized client relationships through proactive outreach, personalized communication, and tailored service offerings that address individual client needs, preferences, and financial goals.

2. Value-added Services: Expand service offerings to include value-added services such as tax planning, financial consulting, retirement planning, or estate planning to meet evolving client needs and enhance service value beyond tax preparation.

3. Client Feedback: Encourage client feedback, testimonials, and referrals as indicators of client satisfaction, loyalty, and advocacy for your tax preparation services. Use client insights to refine service offerings, improve service delivery processes, and strengthen client relationships over time.

Conclusion

Managing client expectations is essential for delivering exceptional service, fostering positive client relationships, and achieving client satisfaction in your tax preparation business. By understanding client needs, setting realistic expectations, implementing effective communication strategies, addressing challenges proactively, and cultivating long-term client relationships based on trust and reliability, you can differentiate your services, build a loyal client base, and position your business for sustained success in the competitive tax services industry. Embrace client-centricity, transparency, and continuous improvement to exceed client expectations, drive business growth, and maintain leadership in a dynamic marketplace.

Chapter 22: Marketing Strategies for Your Tax Preparation Business

Welcome to the chapter dedicated to marketing strategies for your tax preparation business! Effective marketing is essential for attracting new clients, building brand awareness, and differentiating your services in the competitive tax services industry. This chapter explores key strategies, best practices, and practical tips to develop and implement successful marketing initiatives that resonate with your target audience and drive business growth.

Understanding Your Target Audience

Understanding your target audience is the first step in developing a successful marketing strategy:

1. Client Segmentation: Identify and segment your target market based on demographics (e.g., age, income level), psychographics (e.g., lifestyle, values), and tax service needs (e.g., individuals, small businesses, corporations). Tailor marketing messages, content, and promotional offers to address specific client preferences and pain points effectively.

2. Client Persona Development: Create client personas that represent your ideal clients, including their goals, challenges, motivations, and preferred communication channels. Use client personas to personalize marketing campaigns, refine messaging strategies, and attract targeted leads that align with your business objectives.

3. Competitive Analysis: Conduct a competitive analysis to assess competitor strengths, weaknesses, service offerings, pricing strategies, and market positioning. Identify unique selling propositions (USPs), competitive advantages, and opportunities to differentiate your tax preparation services and appeal to prospective clients in your target market.

Developing a Strong Brand Identity

Establishing a strong brand identity helps build credibility, trust, and recognition in the marketplace:

1. Brand Positioning: Define your brand positioning based on core values, mission statement, and unique value propositions that differentiate your tax preparation business from competitors. Communicate your brand's expertise, reliability, and client-centric approach to build brand authority and attract client trust.

2. Brand Visuals: Create cohesive brand visuals, including logos, color schemes, typography, and brand aesthetics that reflect your brand personality and resonate with your target audience. Ensure consistency across marketing collaterals, website design, social media profiles, and promotional materials to reinforce brand recognition and recall.

3. Brand Messaging: Develop compelling brand messages and value propositions that communicate the benefits of your tax preparation services, expertise in tax laws, client success stories, and commitment to delivering exceptional service. Craft clear, concise, and persuasive marketing copy that addresses client needs and highlights the value of choosing your services.

Digital Marketing Strategies

Utilize digital marketing channels and tactics to expand reach, engage prospects, and drive client acquisition:

1. Website Optimization: Optimize your website for search engines (SEO) to improve online visibility, organic traffic, and search engine rankings for relevant keywords (e.g., "tax preparation services near me," "CPA services"). Create informative content, landing pages, and service descriptions that resonate with your target audience and encourage conversions.

2. Content Marketing: Develop a content marketing strategy to educate, inform, and engage prospective clients through blog posts, articles, infographics, and educational resources related to tax preparation tips, tax planning strategies, regulatory updates, and financial literacy topics. Share valuable insights, industry expertise, and actionable advice to establish thought leadership and attract qualified leads.

3. Social Media Engagement: Leverage social media platforms (e.g., LinkedIn, Facebook, Twitter) to engage with prospective clients, share valuable content, promote service offerings, and build relationships with your online community. Use targeted social media advertising, sponsored posts, and social media contests to increase brand visibility, drive website traffic, and generate leads.

Client Referral Programs

Develop client referral programs to incentivize satisfied clients to recommend your tax preparation services to their networks:

1. Referral Incentives: Offer referral incentives, discounts, or exclusive rewards to clients who refer new clients to your tax preparation business. Encourage satisfied clients to share positive testimonials, reviews, or case studies that highlight their positive experiences and outcomes with your services.

2. Referral Partnerships: Establish referral partnerships with professionals in related industries (e.g., financial advisors, attorneys, small business consultants) who can refer clients in need of tax preparation services. Build mutually beneficial relationships, exchange referrals, and collaborate on joint marketing initiatives to expand your client base and increase referral opportunities.

3. Client Advocacy: Cultivate client advocacy by delivering exceptional service, exceeding client expectations, and demonstrating a commitment to client success. Encourage satisfied clients to become brand advocates, share their experiences on social media, and participate in client testimonials or case studies that showcase your expertise and service excellence.

Measuring Marketing Effectiveness

Monitor and measure marketing effectiveness to optimize campaigns, track ROI, and refine strategies for continuous improvement:

1. Key Performance Indicators (KPIs): Define and track key performance indicators (KPIs) such as website traffic, conversion rates, lead generation, client acquisition cost (CAC), and client retention rates to assess the impact of your marketing efforts. Analyze KPI data, identify trends, and make data-driven decisions to optimize marketing campaigns and allocate resources effectively.

2. Analytics Tools: Use analytics tools (e.g., Google Analytics, social media insights, email marketing platforms) to gather actionable data, analyze campaign performance, and gain insights into client behavior, engagement patterns, and marketing attribution. Use data analytics to segment audiences, personalize marketing messages, and optimize conversion pathways to maximize marketing ROI.

3. Continuous Optimization: Continuously optimize marketing strategies, test new tactics, and experiment with A/B testing, multivariate testing, or audience segmentation to improve campaign performance and achieve marketing objectives. Adapt to market trends, client feedback, and industry changes to stay competitive and maintain relevance in the evolving landscape of tax services.

Conclusion

Effective marketing strategies are essential for attracting new clients, building brand credibility, and achieving business growth in your tax preparation business. By understanding your target audience, developing a strong brand identity, leveraging digital marketing channels, implementing client referral programs, measuring marketing effectiveness, and optimizing campaigns for continuous improvement, you can enhance market visibility, drive client acquisition, and position your business as a trusted advisor in tax preparation services. Embrace innovation, creativity, and client-centricity to differentiate your services, cultivate client relationships, and achieve long-term success in the competitive marketplace.

Chapter 23: Client Retention Strategies for Your Tax Preparation Business

Welcome to the chapter dedicated to client retention strategies for your tax preparation business! Retaining existing clients is critical for sustaining business growth, maximizing revenue, and building long-term client relationships in the competitive tax services industry. This chapter explores effective strategies, best practices, and practical tips to enhance client retention, deliver exceptional client experiences, and foster client loyalty in your tax preparation business.

Importance of Client Retention

Understanding the importance of client retention is fundamental to building a successful tax preparation business:

1. Business Sustainability: Retaining existing clients reduces reliance on new client acquisition and stabilizes revenue streams, promoting business sustainability and long-term profitability.

2. Client Loyalty: Loyal clients are more likely to recommend your services, provide positive testimonials, and contribute to business growth through repeat business and referrals.

3. Relationship Building: Building strong client relationships based on trust, reliability, and exceptional service fosters client loyalty, enhances brand reputation, and differentiates your tax preparation business in the marketplace.

Personalized Client Experiences

Deliver personalized client experiences to exceed client expectations and enhance satisfaction:

1. Client Needs Assessment: Conduct thorough client needs assessments to understand individual client preferences, financial goals, and service expectations. Tailor service offerings, communication styles, and service delivery methods to meet unique client needs and enhance client satisfaction.

2. Proactive Communication: Maintain regular communication with clients throughout the year, beyond tax season, to provide updates on tax law changes, financial planning opportunities, and personalized tax-saving strategies. Anticipate client questions, address concerns promptly, and demonstrate proactive client engagement to build trust and rapport.

3. Client Feedback Mechanisms: Implement client feedback mechanisms, satisfaction surveys, or client advisory boards to gather insights, evaluate service quality, and identify opportunities for improvement. Use client feedback to refine service offerings, enhance service delivery processes, and strengthen client relationships over time.

Value-added Services and Education

Offer value-added services and educational resources to add value, build expertise, and empower clients:

1. Tax Planning Services: Provide year-round tax planning services, tax strategy sessions, and financial planning consultations to help clients maximize tax deductions, minimize tax liabilities, and achieve long-term financial goals. Offer personalized recommendations, tax-saving tips, and proactive tax planning strategies to demonstrate added value and expertise.

2. Educational Workshops: Host educational workshops, webinars, or seminars on tax law updates, financial literacy topics, retirement planning, and investment strategies to educate clients and empower them with knowledge. Position your tax preparation business as a trusted advisor, industry expert, and resource for informed financial decision-making.

3. Client Resource Center: Develop a client resource center on your website or digital platform with informative articles, tax guides, calculators, and FAQs to provide clients with self-service tools and valuable resources for tax preparation, financial planning, and compliance requirements. Empower clients to access information conveniently, make informed decisions, and navigate tax complexities effectively.

Loyalty Programs and Incentives

Create loyalty programs, incentives, or exclusive offers to reward client loyalty and encourage repeat business:

1. Loyalty Rewards: Offer loyalty rewards, discounts on future services, or referral incentives to clients who renew annual tax preparation services, refer new clients, or participate in client appreciation events. Recognize loyal clients, celebrate milestones, and express appreciation for their continued trust and partnership.

2. Exclusive Benefits: Provide exclusive benefits, VIP services, or priority scheduling for loyal clients to enhance their service experience, demonstrate appreciation, and differentiate their client experience from new clients. Customize service offerings, anticipate client needs, and deliver personalized perks that recognize client loyalty and value long-term relationships.

3. Client Recognition: Recognize client anniversaries, birthdays, or major life events with personalized messages, handwritten notes, or small tokens of appreciation to strengthen personal connections, foster goodwill, and deepen client relationships. Show genuine interest in client well-being, celebrate achievements, and demonstrate your commitment to client-centric service.

Client Retention Metrics and Evaluation

Monitor client retention metrics, evaluate client satisfaction, and measure loyalty to optimize retention strategies:

1. Client Retention Rate: Calculate client retention rate by measuring the percentage of retained clients over a specific period (e.g., annually) to assess the effectiveness of retention strategies and identify areas for improvement.

2. Net Promoter Score (NPS): Implement NPS surveys to measure client loyalty, likelihood to recommend your services, and overall satisfaction levels. Use NPS feedback to prioritize client experience improvements, address detractors' concerns, and leverage promoters' advocacy for business growth.

3. Client Lifetime Value (CLV): Calculate CLV to estimate the total revenue generated from a client over their lifetime with your tax preparation business. Segment clients based on CLV insights, prioritize high-value client relationships, and allocate resources to maximize client retention and lifetime value contributions.

Conclusion

Client retention strategies are essential for fostering client loyalty, sustaining business growth, and achieving long-term success in your tax preparation business. By delivering personalized client experiences, offering value-added services, implementing loyalty programs, and measuring client satisfaction and loyalty metrics, you can enhance client retention rates, strengthen client relationships, and position your business as a trusted advisor in the competitive tax services industry. Embrace client-centricity, continuous improvement, and proactive client engagement to exceed client expectations, drive business growth, and build a loyal client base that fuels sustained success and market leadership.

Chapter 24: Handling Client Complaints and Resolving Issues Effectively

Welcome to the chapter dedicated to handling client complaints and resolving issues effectively in your tax preparation business! Addressing client complaints with professionalism, empathy, and efficiency is crucial for maintaining client satisfaction, preserving client relationships, and upholding the reputation of your business. This chapter explores strategies, best practices, and practical tips to manage client complaints, resolve issues proactively, and turn challenges into opportunities for client satisfaction and business improvement.

Importance of Effective Complaint Management

Understanding the importance of effective complaint management sets the foundation for improving service delivery and client retention:

1. Client Retention: Resolving client complaints promptly and effectively demonstrates commitment to client satisfaction, loyalty, and retention. Addressing client concerns with empathy and professionalism can turn dissatisfied clients into loyal advocates for your business.

2. Reputation Management: Handling client complaints with transparency and accountability safeguards your business reputation, enhances brand credibility, and differentiates your tax preparation services in the competitive marketplace.

3. Continuous Improvement: Analyzing client feedback and resolving issues proactively allows you to identify systemic issues, implement corrective actions, and improve service delivery processes to prevent future complaints and enhance overall client experience.

Establishing a Complaint Management Framework

Developing a structured complaint management framework helps streamline processes and ensure consistency in handling client complaints:

1. Complaint Reporting: Establish clear procedures for clients to report complaints, issues, or concerns through multiple channels (e.g., phone, email, website). Provide accessible contact information, complaint forms, or online portals for clients to submit feedback and initiate resolution processes.

2. Complaint Triage: Prioritize and categorize client complaints based on severity, impact on client satisfaction, and urgency for resolution. Assign responsibility to designated staff members or complaint resolution teams to investigate, address, and resolve client issues promptly and effectively.

3. Documentation and Tracking: Maintain detailed records of client complaints, including nature of complaint, client contact information, resolution actions taken, and outcomes. Use complaint tracking systems or CRM software to monitor complaint status, follow-up actions, and ensure timely resolution and client communication.

Effective Communication Strategies

Implementing effective communication strategies enhances transparency, builds trust, and facilitates resolution of client complaints:

1. Active Listening: Practice active listening to understand client concerns, acknowledge emotions, and gather relevant information to address root causes of complaints effectively. Demonstrate empathy, patience, and attentiveness to client perspectives to build rapport and trust during complaint resolution.

2. Transparent Communication: Communicate openly and transparently with clients about the status of their complaints, investigation findings, resolution options, and proposed solutions. Keep clients informed of progress, timelines for resolution, and any challenges or barriers encountered during the process.

3. Timely Follow-up: Provide timely updates, follow-up communications, and resolution outcomes to clients throughout the complaint resolution process. Ensure clients feel valued, respected, and informed of actions taken to address their concerns and improve their overall experience with your tax preparation business.

Resolving Complaints with Empathy and Solutions

Resolve client complaints with empathy, professionalism, and client-focused solutions to restore confidence and satisfaction:

1. Root Cause Analysis: Conduct thorough root cause analysis to identify underlying issues, process gaps, or miscommunications that contributed to client complaints. Address systemic issues, implement corrective actions, and streamline processes to prevent recurrence of similar complaints in the future.

2. Client-Centric Solutions: Tailor solutions, remedies, or compensation options to meet client expectations, address grievances, and demonstrate commitment to resolving complaints satisfactorily. Offer personalized resolutions, refunds, service credits, or complimentary services as appropriate to rectify client dissatisfaction and retain client loyalty.

3. Apology and Appreciation: Extend sincere apologies to clients for any inconvenience, dissatisfaction, or service shortcomings they experienced. Express appreciation for their feedback, patience, and continued trust in your tax preparation business while reaffirming your commitment to delivering exceptional service and addressing client concerns effectively.

Learning and Improvement

Embrace client feedback as an opportunity for learning, improvement, and business growth:

1. Continuous Feedback Loop: Encourage ongoing client feedback, suggestions for improvement, and testimonials to evaluate service quality, identify areas for enhancement, and prioritize client-centric initiatives. Use feedback analytics, client surveys, or focus groups to gather actionable insights and drive continuous improvement efforts.

2. Staff Training and Development: Provide training, coaching, and professional development opportunities for staff members to enhance communication skills, conflict resolution techniques, and client relationship management. Equip team members with tools, resources, and best practices for handling client complaints effectively and fostering positive client interactions.

3. Service Excellence Culture: Foster a culture of service excellence, accountability, and continuous improvement within your tax preparation business. Empower staff to take ownership of client satisfaction, uphold service standards, and collaborate cross-functionally to implement process improvements and enhance client experiences proactively.

Conclusion

Handling client complaints and resolving issues effectively is essential for maintaining client satisfaction, preserving client relationships, and achieving business success in your tax preparation business. By establishing a complaint management framework, implementing effective communication strategies, resolving complaints with empathy and solutions, and embracing client feedback for learning and improvement, you can strengthen client trust, enhance service delivery, and differentiate your business in the competitive marketplace. Embrace transparency, accountability, and a client-centric approach to turn challenges into opportunities for client satisfaction, loyalty, and long-term business growth.

Chapter 25: Scaling Your Tax Preparation Business for Growth

Welcome to the chapter dedicated to scaling your tax preparation business for growth! Scaling your business involves strategically expanding operations, increasing client base, optimizing workflows, and enhancing service delivery to accommodate growth opportunities and achieve long-term success in the competitive tax services industry. This chapter explores key strategies, best practices, and practical tips to scale your tax preparation business effectively while maintaining service quality, client satisfaction, and operational efficiency.

Assessing Readiness for Growth

Assessing your readiness for growth sets the foundation for strategic planning and expansion initiatives:

1. Market Analysis: Conduct a thorough market analysis to identify growth opportunities, client demand trends, competitor landscape, and emerging market segments within the tax preparation industry. Evaluate market saturation, regulatory changes, and economic factors that may impact business growth and expansion strategies.

2. Financial Health: Evaluate financial performance, profitability margins, cash flow projections, and capital requirements to support business growth initiatives. Assess financial stability, funding options, and investment opportunities to fund expansion efforts, acquire new clients, and invest in technology infrastructure.

3. Operational Capacity: Evaluate operational capacity, staffing levels, technology infrastructure, and scalability of current processes to support increased client volume, service delivery demands, and operational efficiencies. Identify operational bottlenecks, streamline workflows, and implement scalable solutions to accommodate business growth effectively.

Developing a Growth Strategy

Developing a growth strategy involves setting clear objectives, defining growth initiatives, and aligning resources to achieve business expansion goals:

1. Strategic Planning: Define long-term business goals, growth objectives, and milestones for expanding service offerings, geographic reach, or client segments. Develop a comprehensive growth strategy with actionable initiatives, timelines, and performance metrics to measure progress and success.

2. Service Diversification: Expand service offerings to include complementary services such as tax planning, financial consulting, audit representation, or business advisory services. Diversify revenue streams, cater to diverse client needs, and enhance service value to attract new clients and retain existing clientele.

3. Geographic Expansion: Explore opportunities for geographic expansion into new markets, regions, or demographic areas with underserved client populations. Conduct market research, assess competitive dynamics, and establish local presence through partnerships, satellite offices, or virtual service delivery models.

Leveraging Technology and Automation

Harnessing technology and automation enhances operational efficiency, service delivery, and client engagement in a scalable business environment:

1. Tax Software Integration: Invest in advanced tax preparation software, cloud-based platforms, and digital tools to streamline tax filing processes, automate data entry, and enhance accuracy in preparing client tax returns. Leverage AI-powered solutions, predictive analytics, and machine learning algorithms to optimize tax workflows and improve service efficiency.

2. Client Relationship Management (CRM): Implement a CRM system to manage client interactions, track client preferences, and personalize service delivery. Utilize CRM analytics, client segmentation, and personalized communication strategies to nurture client relationships, anticipate client needs, and enhance client retention rates.

3. Workflow Optimization: Streamline internal workflows, standardize operating procedures, and eliminate redundant tasks to improve productivity, minimize errors, and optimize resource allocation. Adopt lean management principles, agile methodologies, and continuous process improvement strategies to enhance operational agility and scalability.

Talent Acquisition and Development

Attracting top talent, nurturing employee growth, and building a high-performing team are critical for supporting business growth and service excellence:

1. Talent Recruitment: Recruit skilled tax professionals, certified public accountants (CPAs), enrolled agents, and financial experts with expertise in tax law, regulatory compliance, and client service excellence. Develop recruitment strategies, offer competitive compensation packages, and promote your employer brand to attract top talent.

2. Professional Development: Invest in ongoing training, professional development programs, and certifications for staff members to enhance technical skills, industry knowledge, and client service capabilities. Foster a culture of learning, mentorship, and career advancement opportunities to retain talent and build a high-performing workforce.

3. Team Collaboration: Promote cross-functional collaboration, teamwork, and knowledge sharing among staff members to leverage collective expertise, solve complex client challenges, and deliver integrated solutions. Encourage a collaborative work environment, open communication channels, and teamwork to foster innovation and drive business growth.

Monitoring and Adaptation

Monitor key performance indicators (KPIs), client feedback, and market trends to evaluate growth strategies, adapt to changing business dynamics, and drive continuous improvement:

1. Performance Metrics: Track KPIs such as client acquisition cost (CAC), client retention rate, revenue growth, profitability margins, and client satisfaction scores to measure the effectiveness of growth strategies and identify areas for improvement.

2. Client Feedback: Gather client feedback through satisfaction surveys, testimonials, and client advisory boards to assess service quality, identify client needs, and enhance service delivery. Use client insights to refine service offerings, address client concerns, and strengthen client relationships.

3. Agility and Flexibility: Maintain flexibility, agility, and responsiveness to adapt to market changes, regulatory updates, and client preferences. Anticipate industry trends, competitive pressures, and economic shifts to pivot strategies, reallocate resources, and seize growth opportunities in a dynamic business environment.

Conclusion

Scaling your tax preparation business for growth requires strategic planning, operational readiness, technological innovation, talent development, and a client-centric approach to service delivery. By assessing readiness for growth, developing a growth strategy, leveraging technology and automation, nurturing talent, and monitoring performance metrics, you can expand business operations, attract new clients, enhance service capabilities, and achieve sustainable growth in the competitive tax services industry. Embrace innovation, adaptability, and a commitment to excellence to position your business for long-term success and leadership in the evolving marketplace.

Chapter 26: Managing Seasonal Fluctuations in Your Tax Preparation Business

Welcome to the chapter dedicated to managing seasonal fluctuations in your tax preparation business! Seasonal fluctuations, particularly during tax season, pose unique challenges and opportunities for tax preparation firms. This chapter explores strategies, best practices, and practical tips to effectively manage workload variability, optimize operational efficiency, maintain service quality, and capitalize on peak periods in the tax services industry.

Understanding Seasonal Fluctuations

Understanding the nature and impact of seasonal fluctuations is essential for planning and preparation:

1. Tax Filing Deadlines: Recognize peak periods during tax season, including key filing deadlines such as April 15 for individual tax returns and March 15 for business tax returns. Anticipate increased client demand, workload intensity, and operational pressures during peak filing periods.

2. Client Behavior: Analyze client behavior and trends, including procrastination tendencies, early filers, and seasonal fluctuations in client inquiries, appointments, and service requests. Monitor client engagement patterns, appointment scheduling trends, and service delivery preferences during peak and off-peak periods.

3. Industry Dynamics: Consider industry dynamics, regulatory changes, economic factors, and external influences (e.g., tax law reforms, economic downturns) that may impact client demand, service volumes, and operational capacity during tax season and throughout the year.

Preparing for Peak Season

Preparation is key to managing seasonal fluctuations and optimizing service delivery during peak periods:

1. Staffing Strategy: Develop a staffing strategy to meet increased client demand during peak tax season. Hire seasonal staff, certified public accountants (CPAs), enrolled agents, or temporary professionals with tax preparation expertise to augment workforce capacity and support service delivery requirements.

2. Training and Readiness: Provide comprehensive training, onboarding programs, and continuing education for staff members to enhance tax preparation skills, knowledge of tax law updates, and proficiency in using tax preparation software. Ensure staff readiness, competence, and adherence to service standards during peak workload periods.

3. Resource Allocation: Allocate resources effectively, including office space, technology infrastructure, tax preparation software licenses, and client communication tools, to support increased service volumes, workflow efficiency, and client engagement during peak season.

Enhancing Operational Efficiency

Optimizing operational efficiency streamlines processes, minimizes bottlenecks, and improves service delivery capabilities:

1. Workflow Management: Implement workflow management systems, standardized procedures, and task prioritization strategies to streamline tax preparation processes, manage client caseloads, and ensure timely completion of tax returns during peak periods.

2. Technology Integration: Leverage advanced tax preparation software, cloud-based platforms, and digital tools to automate data entry, streamline document management, and enhance collaboration among team members. Utilize predictive analytics, machine learning algorithms, and AI-powered solutions to optimize tax workflows and improve accuracy.

3. Client Communication: Maintain proactive communication with clients regarding appointment scheduling, document submission deadlines, tax filing status updates, and service expectations during peak season. Utilize automated reminders, client portals, and digital communication channels to facilitate seamless client interactions and minimize communication delays.

Managing Client Expectations

Managing client expectations promotes transparency, builds trust, and enhances client satisfaction during peak workload periods:

1. Service Agreements: Establish clear service agreements, engagement terms, and expectations with clients regarding service delivery timelines, fee structures, document requirements, and communication protocols during tax season.

2. Realistic Timelines: Set realistic turnaround times for tax preparation services, client consultations, and document review processes to manage client expectations, prioritize workload assignments, and ensure quality control measures are maintained.

3. Client Education: Educate clients on tax filing deadlines, documentation requirements, tax law changes, and potential tax implications to empower informed decision-making, facilitate timely compliance, and minimize last-minute filing challenges during peak season.

Post-Season Evaluation and Reflection

Conducting post-season evaluation and reflection enables continuous improvement and preparation for future seasonal fluctuations:

1. Performance Review: Evaluate key performance indicators (KPIs), client satisfaction scores, service delivery metrics, and operational efficiencies achieved during peak season. Identify strengths, challenges, and areas for improvement in service delivery, client management, and operational effectiveness.

2. Staff Feedback: Gather feedback from staff members, seasonal hires, and client-facing teams regarding their experiences, challenges encountered, and suggestions for process enhancements or workflow improvements during peak workload periods.

3. Strategic Planning: Develop strategic plans, contingency strategies, and operational readiness initiatives based on lessons learned, client feedback, industry trends, and anticipated changes in client demand for future tax seasons. Implement proactive measures, staff training programs, and technology upgrades to enhance readiness and responsiveness to seasonal fluctuations.

Conclusion

Managing seasonal fluctuations in your tax preparation business requires proactive planning, strategic preparation, operational efficiency, and client-centric service delivery to navigate peak periods effectively and capitalize on business opportunities. By understanding seasonal dynamics, preparing for peak season, optimizing operational efficiency, managing client expectations, and conducting post-season evaluation, you can enhance service quality, maintain client satisfaction, and achieve sustainable growth in the competitive tax services industry. Embrace flexibility, adaptability, and a commitment to excellence to successfully manage seasonal fluctuations and position your business for long-term success and profitability.

Chapter 27: Building Strategic Partnerships in Your Tax Preparation Business

Welcome to the chapter dedicated to building strategic partnerships in your tax preparation business! Strategic partnerships play a crucial role in expanding service capabilities, accessing new client markets, and driving business growth in the competitive tax services industry. This chapter explores the benefits of strategic partnerships, key considerations for partnership development, and practical strategies to establish and leverage partnerships effectively for mutual success and client satisfaction.

Understanding Strategic Partnerships

Understanding the significance of strategic partnerships sets the stage for collaborative growth and enhanced service offerings:

1. Partnership Benefits: Strategic partnerships offer opportunities to complement service offerings, expand market reach, access specialized expertise, and leverage shared resources for mutual business growth and competitive advantage.

2. Collaboration Opportunities: Collaborate with industry peers, complementary service providers, financial institutions, or technology companies to offer integrated solutions, cross-referral opportunities, and value-added services that meet diverse client needs and preferences.

3. Relationship Building: Build trust, foster collaboration, and cultivate long-term relationships with strategic partners based on shared values, mutual goals, and a commitment to delivering exceptional client outcomes and service excellence.

Identifying Strategic Partnership Opportunities

Identifying potential strategic partners involves evaluating industry alignment, client demographics, and shared business objectives:

1. Market Research: Conduct market research, competitor analysis, and industry trends to identify potential strategic partners with complementary service offerings, industry expertise, and a client base that aligns with your tax preparation business goals.

2. Client Needs Assessment: Assess client needs, preferences, and emerging trends in tax services, financial planning, or business advisory services to identify partnership opportunities that enhance service value, address client pain points, and differentiate your service offerings in the marketplace.

3. Networking and Referrals: Network with industry associations, professional networks, and business forums to connect with potential strategic partners, exchange referrals, and explore collaboration opportunities based on shared interests, industry reputation, and client-centric service delivery.

Developing Strategic Partnerships

Developing strategic partnerships requires effective communication, collaboration, and alignment of business objectives:

1. Partnership Alignment: Establish clear objectives, mutual expectations, and alignment of business goals with strategic partners to ensure shared commitment, accountability, and a collaborative approach to achieving mutual success and client satisfaction.

2. Partnership Agreements: Draft partnership agreements, formalize terms of engagement, and define roles, responsibilities, and performance metrics for measuring partnership effectiveness, client referrals, revenue sharing, and service delivery standards.

3. Value Proposition: Articulate your unique value proposition, service differentiation, and competitive advantages to prospective strategic partners. Highlight synergies, mutual benefits, and opportunities for cross-promotion, client acquisition, and market expansion through collaborative efforts.

Leveraging Partner Resources and Expertise

Leveraging partner resources and expertise enhances service capabilities, client satisfaction, and business growth:

1. Service Integration: Integrate partner solutions, technology platforms, or specialized expertise into your service offerings to enhance service breadth, operational efficiency, and client value proposition. Offer comprehensive solutions, bundled services, or value-added packages that meet diverse client needs and exceed expectations.

2. Cross-Referral Programs: Implement cross-referral programs, joint marketing initiatives, and co-branded campaigns with strategic partners to generate leads, expand client reach, and foster client loyalty through shared promotional efforts and client endorsements.

3. Client Education and Support: Collaborate with strategic partners to provide client education seminars, workshops, or webinars on tax planning, financial literacy, retirement planning, and investment strategies. Empower clients with knowledge, resources, and personalized advice to make informed financial decisions and achieve their financial goals.

Monitoring and Measuring Partnership Success

Monitoring and measuring partnership success involves evaluating performance metrics, client feedback, and business outcomes:

1. Performance Metrics: Track key performance indicators (KPIs), client acquisition rates, referral conversion rates, revenue growth, and client satisfaction scores attributed to strategic partnerships. Assess partnership ROI, profitability margins, and long-term value generated for both parties.

2. Client Feedback: Gather client feedback, testimonials, and satisfaction surveys to evaluate partnership impact on service quality, client experience, and perceived value. Use client insights to refine partnership strategies, address client needs, and enhance collaborative efforts for continuous improvement.

3. Partnership Evolution: Foster ongoing communication, collaboration, and relationship-building activities with strategic partners. Adapt partnership strategies, explore new growth opportunities, and evolve partnership agreements based on changing market dynamics, client preferences, and industry trends to sustain partnership longevity and mutual success.

Conclusion

Building strategic partnerships in your tax preparation business is essential for expanding service capabilities, accessing new client markets, and driving business growth through collaborative efforts, shared resources, and mutual expertise. By understanding partnership benefits, identifying opportunities, developing collaborative relationships, leveraging partner resources, and monitoring partnership success, you can enhance service differentiation, client satisfaction, and market competitiveness in the dynamic landscape of tax services. Embrace collaboration, innovation, and a client-centric approach to building strategic partnerships that foster mutual success, sustainable growth, and industry leadership in the competitive marketplace.

Chapter 28: Navigating Tax Compliance and Regulatory Changes

Welcome to the chapter dedicated to navigating tax compliance and regulatory changes in your tax preparation business! Staying informed and compliant with tax laws, regulations, and legislative changes is essential for ensuring accuracy, minimizing risks, and maintaining client trust in the dynamic tax services industry. This chapter explores strategies, best practices, and practical tips to navigate tax compliance requirements, adapt to regulatory changes, and uphold professional standards in delivering quality tax preparation services.

Importance of Tax Compliance

Understanding the importance of tax compliance sets the foundation for ethical practice and client service excellence:

1. Legal Obligations: Comply with federal, state, and local tax laws, regulations, filing deadlines, and reporting requirements to avoid penalties, legal liabilities, and reputational risks for your tax preparation business and clients.

2. Client Trust: Demonstrate integrity, transparency, and adherence to professional standards in tax preparation services to build and maintain client trust, loyalty, and long-term client relationships.

3. Ethical Practice: Uphold ethical standards, confidentiality obligations, and fiduciary responsibilities in handling sensitive client information, financial data, and tax-related disclosures with utmost professionalism and discretion.

Staying Informed about Regulatory Changes

Staying informed about regulatory changes is crucial for proactive compliance and informed decision-making:

1. Regulatory Updates: Monitor tax law updates, legislative changes, regulatory amendments, and IRS announcements affecting tax preparation practices, filing requirements, deduction limits, credits, and compliance obligations for individual and business taxpayers.

2. Professional Development: Participate in continuing education programs, tax seminars, industry webinars, and professional conferences to stay abreast of regulatory developments, industry trends, best practices, and emerging tax issues impacting client tax returns and financial planning strategies.

3. Resource Utilization: Utilize tax research tools, authoritative publications, IRS guidance documents, and industry resources (e.g., tax manuals, technical bulletins) to interpret complex tax provisions, navigate regulatory uncertainties, and provide accurate tax advice and compliance solutions to clients.

Implementing Effective Compliance Practices

Implementing effective compliance practices ensures consistency, accuracy, and diligence in tax preparation services:

1. Compliance Checklist: Develop a comprehensive compliance checklist outlining key tax filing requirements, documentation standards, verification procedures, and due diligence practices to mitigate errors, omissions, and regulatory non-compliance in client tax returns.

2. Quality Control: Establish robust quality control measures, peer review processes, and internal audits to review tax returns, identify potential errors, inconsistencies, or compliance issues, and ensure adherence to professional standards, IRS guidelines, and regulatory mandates.

3. Client Communication: Educate clients on tax compliance responsibilities, filing deadlines, record-keeping requirements, and potential tax implications to promote proactive tax planning, accurate reporting, and compliance with changing tax laws and regulatory requirements.

Leveraging Technology for Compliance

Harnessing technology enhances efficiency, accuracy, and compliance in tax preparation processes:

1. Tax Preparation Software: Invest in advanced tax preparation software, cloud-based platforms, and digital tools equipped with built-in compliance checks, data validation features, and automated updates to streamline tax calculations, minimize filing errors, and ensure regulatory compliance.

2. Data Security: Implement robust cybersecurity measures, data encryption protocols, and secure file sharing systems to protect client data, confidential information, and sensitive financial records from unauthorized access, cyber threats, and data breaches.

3. Electronic Filing: Utilize electronic filing options, IRS e-Services, and secure portals to submit accurate tax returns, track filing status, receive acknowledgments, and comply with IRS e-file mandates for faster processing, confirmation, and compliance verification.

Proactive Risk Management

Proactive risk management strategies mitigate compliance risks, operational vulnerabilities, and regulatory challenges:

1. Risk Assessment: Conduct periodic risk assessments, compliance audits, and due diligence reviews to assess regulatory compliance, identify potential tax liabilities, and implement corrective actions, controls, or remedial measures to mitigate compliance risks.

2. Legal Counsel: Consult with legal advisors, tax attorneys, or compliance specialists to seek professional guidance, interpret complex tax regulations, navigate regulatory uncertainties, and resolve compliance issues impacting client tax preparation services and business operations.

3. Continuous Improvement: Foster a culture of continuous improvement, professional development, and regulatory compliance within your tax preparation business. Stay proactive, adaptive, and responsive to regulatory changes, client feedback, industry trends, and emerging tax issues to enhance service delivery, client satisfaction, and business resilience.

Conclusion

Navigating tax compliance and regulatory changes in your tax preparation business requires vigilance, expertise, and commitment to ethical practice, client service excellence, and regulatory compliance. By understanding the importance of tax compliance, staying informed about regulatory changes, implementing effective compliance practices, leveraging technology, and adopting proactive risk management strategies, you can uphold professional standards, minimize compliance risks, and deliver reliable tax preparation services that meet client expectations and regulatory requirements. Embrace diligence, expertise, and a client-centric approach to navigating tax compliance challenges and positioning your tax preparation business for long-term success and industry leadership in the evolving landscape of tax services.

Chapter 29: Enhancing Client Relationships in Your Tax Preparation Business

Welcome to the chapter dedicated to enhancing client relationships in your tax preparation business! Building strong, long-lasting relationships with clients is essential for client satisfaction, retention, and business growth in the competitive tax services industry. This chapter explores strategies, best practices, and practical tips to cultivate meaningful client relationships, deliver exceptional client experiences, and foster client loyalty through personalized service, communication excellence, and proactive client engagement.

Importance of Client Relationships

Understanding the significance of client relationships sets the foundation for client-centric service delivery and business success:

1. Client Trust: Build trust, credibility, and rapport with clients through transparent communication, ethical conduct, and personalized attention to their tax planning, preparation, and financial needs.

2. Client Loyalty: Foster client loyalty, repeat business, and referrals by delivering high-quality service, exceeding client expectations, and demonstrating commitment to their financial well-being and tax compliance requirements.

3. Business Growth: Strengthen client relationships to drive business growth, expand service offerings, and differentiate your tax preparation business in the marketplace through positive client testimonials, word-of-mouth referrals, and client advocacy.

Understanding Client Needs and Preferences

Understanding client needs and preferences enables personalized service delivery and client-centric solutions:

1. Client Segmentation: Segment clients based on demographics, life stages, financial goals, and tax complexity to tailor service offerings, communication strategies, and service delivery models that meet diverse client needs and preferences.

2. Client Consultations: Conduct comprehensive client consultations, needs assessments, and financial reviews to identify client priorities, tax planning objectives, and opportunities to provide value-added services that optimize tax savings and financial outcomes.

3. Communication Channels: Utilize multiple communication channels, including face-to-face meetings, virtual consultations, email communications, and client portals, to engage clients, provide timely updates, address inquiries, and foster proactive communication throughout the tax preparation process.

Delivering Exceptional Client Experiences

Delivering exceptional client experiences enhances satisfaction, loyalty, and advocacy:

1. Service Excellence: Strive for service excellence by delivering accurate, timely, and comprehensive tax preparation services, adhering to professional standards, and exceeding client expectations in service delivery and client outcomes.

2. Personalized Attention: Provide personalized attention, proactive tax advice, and tailored solutions that address client-specific tax concerns, financial goals, and long-term planning objectives to enhance client satisfaction and loyalty.

3. Client Education: Empower clients with knowledge, resources, and educational materials on tax law updates, deduction strategies, retirement planning, and financial literacy to promote informed decision-making and proactive tax planning throughout the year.

Building Client Trust and Confidence

Building client trust and confidence requires integrity, transparency, and professionalism:

1. Transparent Communication: Communicate openly, honestly, and transparently with clients regarding service fees, engagement terms, tax implications, and regulatory changes to build trust, manage expectations, and mitigate misunderstandings.

2. Ethical Conduct: Uphold ethical standards, confidentiality obligations, and fiduciary responsibilities in handling sensitive client information, financial data, and tax-related disclosures with integrity, professionalism, and discretion.

3. Client Feedback: Seek client feedback, testimonials, and satisfaction surveys to evaluate service quality, client perceptions, and areas for improvement in service delivery, communication effectiveness, and client relationship management.

Enhancing Client Engagement and Retention

Enhancing client engagement and retention fosters long-term relationships and business sustainability:

1. Relationship Management: Implement client relationship management (CRM) systems, client engagement strategies, and personalized follow-up initiatives to nurture client relationships, maintain regular contact, and anticipate client needs throughout the year.

2. Value-Added Services: Offer value-added services such as tax planning consultations, financial advisory services, retirement planning strategies, and educational workshops to add value, differentiate your service offerings, and deepen client engagement and loyalty.

3. Client Appreciation: Express gratitude, recognize client milestones, and celebrate client achievements through personalized gestures, holiday greetings, client appreciation events, and loyalty rewards programs to reinforce client loyalty and strengthen business relationships.

Continuous Improvement and Client-Centric Innovation

Continuous improvement and client-centric innovation drive service excellence and business growth:

1. Feedback Utilization: Utilize client feedback, performance metrics, and service evaluations to identify opportunities for service enhancement, process improvements, and innovation in client service delivery and relationship management.

2. Technology Integration: Leverage advanced technology, digital tools, and automation solutions to streamline client interactions, enhance service efficiency, and deliver personalized client experiences through online portals, mobile applications, and virtual service options.

3. Professional Development: Invest in ongoing training, professional development programs, and industry certifications for staff members to enhance client relationship management skills, client service excellence, and technical proficiency in tax preparation and financial advisory services.

Conclusion

Enhancing client relationships in your tax preparation business is essential for fostering client trust, satisfaction, and loyalty through personalized service, communication excellence, and proactive client engagement. By understanding the importance of client relationships, understanding client needs and preferences, delivering exceptional client experiences, building client trust and confidence, enhancing client engagement and retention, and embracing continuous improvement and client-centric innovation, you can cultivate meaningful client relationships, drive business growth, and achieve long-term success in the competitive tax services industry. Embrace client-centricity, integrity, and a commitment to excellence in client relationship management to differentiate your tax preparation business and become a trusted advisor and partner in your clients' financial success.

Chapter 30: Expanding Your Tax Preparation Business: Strategies for Growth and Scalability

Welcome to the chapter dedicated to expanding your tax preparation business! As your tax preparation business matures, expanding your client base, increasing revenue streams, and scaling operations become key objectives for sustainable growth and long-term success. This chapter explores strategies, best practices, and practical tips to expand your tax preparation business, optimize operational efficiency, diversify service offerings, and capitalize on growth opportunities in the competitive tax services industry.

Assessing Readiness for Expansion

Assessing your readiness for expansion sets the foundation for strategic growth planning and implementation:

1. Business Analysis: Conduct a comprehensive business analysis, including financial performance review, client demographics analysis, market positioning assessment, and competitive landscape evaluation to identify growth opportunities, operational strengths, and areas for improvement.

2. Scalability Assessment: Evaluate scalability factors, including organizational structure, staffing capabilities, technology infrastructure, and operational processes, to determine readiness to accommodate increased client demand, service volumes, and business expansion initiatives.

3. Market Research: Conduct market research, client surveys, and industry trend analysis to identify emerging market opportunities, client needs, and competitive threats that influence expansion strategies, service differentiation, and value proposition development in the tax services marketplace.

Developing a Growth Strategy

Developing a growth strategy involves setting clear objectives, defining actionable goals, and prioritizing strategic initiatives:

1. Goal Setting: Set SMART (Specific, Measurable, Achievable, Relevant, Time-bound) goals for business growth, revenue targets, client acquisition rates, market penetration, and service expansion initiatives to guide decision-making and measure progress towards achieving strategic objectives.

2. Service Diversification: Diversify service offerings, including tax planning, financial advisory services, retirement planning, business consulting, and specialized industry expertise to expand service capabilities, attract new client segments, and generate additional revenue streams.

3. Geographic Expansion: Explore geographic expansion opportunities by targeting new market segments, expanding service coverage areas, establishing satellite offices, or leveraging virtual service options to reach a broader client base and enhance market penetration in underserved regions.

Strengthening Operational Infrastructure

Strengthening operational infrastructure enhances efficiency, scalability, and service delivery capabilities:

1. Technology Investment: Invest in advanced tax preparation software, cloud-based platforms, digital tools, and automation solutions to streamline workflow processes, enhance data security, improve client engagement, and optimize operational efficiency in service delivery and client management.

2. Staff Development: Develop talent acquisition strategies, professional development programs, and training initiatives to recruit skilled professionals, enhance staff competencies in tax preparation, financial advisory services, and client relationship management, and foster a culture of continuous learning, innovation, and service excellence.

3. Process Optimization: Implement process optimization initiatives, standard operating procedures (SOPs), and quality assurance protocols to standardize service delivery, minimize operational inefficiencies, and maintain service consistency across multiple locations or service channels.

Leveraging Strategic Partnerships

Leveraging strategic partnerships enhances service capabilities, client value proposition, and market competitiveness:

1. Partner Collaboration: Collaborate with strategic partners, industry alliances, financial institutions, or technology providers to offer integrated solutions, cross-referral opportunities, and value-added services that address client needs, enhance service differentiation, and expand service delivery capabilities.

2. Joint Marketing Initiatives: Develop joint marketing campaigns, co-branded promotions, and referral programs with strategic partners to generate leads, increase client acquisition rates, and amplify brand visibility in target markets through shared marketing efforts, client endorsements, and networking opportunities.

3. Client Acquisition: Implement client acquisition strategies, client retention programs, and client referral incentives to attract new clients, retain existing clients, and maximize client lifetime value through personalized service, proactive communication, and tailored solutions that meet client needs and exceed expectations.

Monitoring Growth Metrics and Performance

Monitoring growth metrics and performance indicators enables strategic decision-making and course correction:

1. Performance Monitoring: Track key performance indicators (KPIs), financial metrics, client acquisition rates, revenue growth, client satisfaction scores, and operational efficiency benchmarks to assess business performance, measure progress towards growth goals, and identify areas for improvement or strategic intervention.

2. Client Feedback: Solicit client feedback, testimonials, and satisfaction surveys to evaluate service quality, client perceptions, and overall client satisfaction with expanded service offerings, service delivery experiences, and client relationship management practices.

3. Strategic Adaptation: Adapt growth strategies, operational tactics, and business expansion initiatives based on market feedback, client preferences, industry trends, and competitive dynamics to optimize business performance, sustain growth momentum, and achieve long-term success in the competitive tax services industry.

Conclusion

Expanding your tax preparation business requires strategic planning, operational readiness, and a client-centric approach to capitalize on growth opportunities, optimize service delivery, and achieve sustainable business success. By assessing readiness for expansion, developing a growth strategy, strengthening operational infrastructure, leveraging strategic partnerships, monitoring growth metrics, and adapting strategies based on market dynamics and client feedback, you can expand your tax preparation business, enhance client satisfaction, and position your firm as a trusted advisor and industry leader in the competitive marketplace. Embrace innovation, strategic collaboration, and a commitment to excellence in service delivery to drive business growth, client loyalty, and profitability in the evolving landscape of tax services.

Conclusion: Your Path to Success in Starting a Tax Preparation Business

Congratulations on reaching the conclusion of this comprehensive guide on starting a tax preparation business! Throughout this book, we've explored every aspect of launching, running, and expanding your tax services venture. From initial planning and legal considerations to marketing strategies, operational efficiencies, client management, and strategic growth initiatives, you've gained valuable insights and practical advice to navigate the complexities of the tax services industry.

Starting a tax preparation business is not just about crunching numbers—it's about building trust, delivering exceptional client experiences, and staying ahead in a competitive market. As you embark on this journey, remember that success lies in your commitment to excellence, integrity in client relationships, and continuous learning and adaptation to industry changes.

Reflecting on Your Journey:

- **Foundational Knowledge:** You've acquired a solid foundation in tax law, regulatory compliance, and business operations critical for establishing your business's credibility and client trust.
- **Client-Centric Approach:** Embracing a client-centric approach ensures that every interaction with your clients is personalized, transparent, and focused on their unique financial needs and goals.
- **Operational Excellence:** Implementing efficient workflows, leveraging technology, and nurturing a skilled team are key to delivering consistent, high-quality services that exceed client expectations.

- **Strategic Growth:** From identifying market opportunities to expanding your service offerings and forming strategic partnerships, you're poised to grow sustainably and scale your business effectively.

Best Wishes for Success:

As you apply the knowledge and strategies from this book, remember that every challenge is an opportunity for growth, and every client interaction is a chance to demonstrate your expertise and dedication. Your passion for helping clients navigate tax complexities and achieve financial peace of mind will be the cornerstone of your success.

Final Thoughts:

With my best wishes for your success in starting and growing your tax preparation business, may you thrive in providing valuable services, building lasting client relationships, and making a meaningful impact in your community. Stay resilient, innovative, and committed to excellence, and your journey in the tax services industry will be both rewarding and fulfilling.

Here's to your bright future as a trusted tax advisor and entrepreneur!

Best regards,

www.ingramcontent.com/pod-product-compliance
Lightning Source LLC
Chambersburg PA
CBHW071930210526
45479CB00002B/623